bocaditos

The Little Dishes of Mexico

by Reed Hearon

Photographs by Laurie Smith

CHRONICLE BOOKS

SAN FRANCISCO

Library of Congress Cataloging-in-Publication Data:

Hearon, Reed.
Bocaditos: the little dishes of Mexico/by Reed Hearon;
photographs by Laurie Smith.
p. cm.
Includes index.
ISBN 0-8118-1009-7 (pbk.)
1. Appetizers. 2. Cookery, Mexican. I. Title.
TX740.H34 1996
641.8'12—dc20   96-11027
                        CIP

Book Design by Jim Christie.
Printed in Hong Kong.

The photographer wishes to thank her mother for friendship, support, and inspiration.

Distributed in Canada by Raincoast Books
8680 Cambie Street
Vancouver, B.C. V6P 6M9

10 9 8 7 6 5 4 3 2 1

Chronicle Books
85 Second Street
San Francisco, CA 94105

www.chronbooks.com

Fried Squash Blossoms

For the staff at Café Marimba, LuLu, and Rose Pistola for their brilliant performance and hard work. Thanks for teaching me so much. Special thanks to Christy for helping to write the book and to the good folks at Chronicle for bugging me to get it done when I couldn't possibly have done it alone.

Ceviche Tostadas

Contents

Vuelve la Vida

Ancho Chiles with Goat Cheese

Introduction

Mexico eats well. Day and night little bites—bocaditos—nourish the color and warmth of life. They reflect the different phases of the day: a midmorning snack from a charcoal-fired *comal* in the market, the heart of a long, lazy lunch with friends, the kindling that sparks cocktails, the answer to an improbablate-night hunger. Simply put, bocaditos are part of the fabric of life.

Crunchy, spicy, colorful, bocadito means "little mouth" or "little bite." No matter whether you call it a *botana*, *antojito*, or *marisco*, it will fill the little hungers of the day. Alone a bocadito is a snack, a nosh. A few combined make a terrific informal meal. Together they are a fiesta, an evening with friends. What a shame that in the United States we have eradicated street food except for the occasional steamed hot dog and canned pop. Bocaditos are spicy, fun to make and eat, and they are the foods most commonly thought of as Mexican food. North of the border we are all familiar with tortilla chips, tacos, and tamales. These are all bocaditos, transformed to fit the mass-market tastes of the United States.

Share with me the delight of preparing these authentic foods. Follow me to a tent in Oaxaca at Christmas as quesadillas are cooked on a clay *comal*. Eat tiny *chiles rellenos* stuffed with cheese, squash blossoms, and even tuna in a stylish Mexico City dining room. Relax on the verandah of an old *fonda* sipping a cold *añejo* and soda and nibbling on crunchy vegetables pickled in pineapple vinegar with a jolt of jalapeño. Watch as corn husks, a raw tortilla, and a bit of *mole* become a fabulously delicate tamale. Join me in Puebla as a ten-year-old boy prepares a chewy, crisp *chalupa* from *masa* and a bit of salsa. Enjoy the crunchy giant tortillas called *tlayudas* with *queso fresco*, or a marvelous ceviche of fresh shucked clams with only a squeeze of lime and a dusting of red chile. Lazily pick up bits of tuna doused with lime and chiles, or crispy pumpkin seeds accented with toasted garlic and fiery chiles. In short, take a little bite of any of these wonderful foods and discover what you are missing.

Ingredients

The authentic flavor of true Mexican food depends on the savor of a wide range of ingredients uncommon to the U.S. larder. Much as sun-dried tomatoes and fresh sweet basil were thought of as exotic in the 1970s, so now are *epazote* and *hierba santa*. You will be rewarded for seeking out these unfamiliar ingredients in the discovery of the breadth and depth of flavor characteristic of Mexican cooking. Most U.S. cities have a Mexican or Latin American grocery store, and the majority of large supermarkets stock a range of Mexican products.

Achiote paste: This slightly spicy blend of the iodiney seeds of the annatto tree, citrus juices, vinegar, and other spices is an all-time favorite for seasoning grilled meats, poultry, and seafood.

Avocado leaves: The heady anise aroma that characterizes much of Oaxacan cookery comes from the avocado leaf.

Banana leaves: The fragrant giant leaf of the banana plant adds an aniselike aroma to foods. Widely available in Asian markets, as well as Mexican and Latin American.

Canela: Widely used in Mexican cooking, this is the soft-bark variety of cinnamon you may remember from Red Hots candies as a child, not the hard-bark variety used in the United States to flavor apple pie.

Chicharrónes: People either love these fried pork skins or hate them. I personally love them, although I confine them to that group of foods, like foie gras and biscuits with butter, that my waistline doesn't allow to be an every-day thing.

Chiles: The two most important things to know about a chile is whether it is fresh or dried and how hot it is. Do not try to modulate the heat in a recipe by varying the quantity of a particular chile. Heat is only one of many flavor components: smoky, sweet, sharp, and astringent are others. If you adjust the amount of a given chile in a dish, you may throw the dish out of balance. If the heat bothers you, make a different dish that uses a milder chile.

Fresh chiles

Anaheim: This long, green, mild chile can be a bit anemic in flavor, but is much improved by roasting, particularly over a wood fire.

Chile de Agua: A light green to fiery orange (depending on ripeness) triangular chile that is rather hot and is widely seen in the markets of Oaxaca. Or save the plane fare and call Café Marimba: they'll send you some "water chiles" (see Mail-order Sources).

Güero: When roasted, this greenish yellow chile takes on a rich flavor, more subtle and light than the roasted jalapeño.

Habanero: This small, round chile is reported to be the hottest in the world. Aside from its remarkable heat, it has an elusive floral, citrusy flavor that makes it a highly prized component in many salsas.

Jalapeño: Probably the most familiar and popular hot chile on the market. When using jalapeños, do not remove the seeds unless the recipe calls for it. The seeds themselves have a distinct sharp flavor that is vital to some dishes.

Poblano: Big (about 5 inches), heart shaped, dark green, meaty, and mildly spicy, poblanos are wonderful roasted and, if you are careful and do not overly blacken the skin, you do not have to peel them.

Serrano: This light green, skinny chile with a bright, clean heat and flavor can be significantly hotter than the jalapeño. Always use the seeds. They are vital to the serrano's flavor.

Dried chiles

Ancho: Perhaps the most widely used dried chile in Mexico. Look for soft, flexible anchos that smell fresh, not musty.

Chipotle: This is the dried, ripe version of a particular type of jalapeño and one of my favorite chiles. It's very hot!

Chipotle en Adobo: Chipotle chiles (and, confusingly, the morita chile) are widely sold canned as *chiles chipotles en adobo*. They are delicious by themselves as a condiment, and may be used as you would Tabasco sauce.

Guajillo: This is the dried version of the Mexican (unhybridized) variety of the New Mexico-type red chile. Use it in conjunction with chipotles for a complex layering of flavor and heat.

Morita: The little brother of the chipotle chile is widely used in Veracruz. It is about $1\frac{1}{2}$ inches long, smoky, and hot.

Oaxacan Pasilla: Grown in Oaxaca, this type of pasilla chile is rolled in hot embers during the drying process to prevent molding.

Pasilla: This is a blackish chile 5 to 8 inches long with a deep cocoalike flavor. Unfortunately, the name *pasilla* is used in parts of the United States to refer not to a dried chile, but instead to the fresh poblano.

Pequin: Pequin means "little" and these round chiles are indeed small; sometimes as many as 25 of them will fit into a tablespoon. But don't be fooled by their size. They're hot.

Corn masa for tortillas: Fresh corn *masa* is readily available from tortilla factories and Mexican groceries in most medium and large cities throughout the United States.

Crema: Mexican soured cream. It is often very hard to find. The perfect substitute is crème fraîche, or mix 3 parts sour cream and 1 part whipping cream.

Spicy Pumpkin Seeds

Dried Mexican oregano: Mexican oregano has a flavor distinct from that of Greek oregano. Greek oregano tastes like pizza, while Mexican oregano tastes like Mexican food. Mexican oregano develops its full flavor when toasted in a dry skillet until fragrant.

Epazote: A deep green herb with serrated leaves and a pungent smell reminiscent of kerosene. It is essential to a wide range of dishes, including a large number of Veracruz specialties, as well as black beans.

Hierba santa: Also known as *hoja santa*, this large, heart-shaped leaf adds an exotic aroma hinting of anise, camphor, or even sassafras to the dishes of Oaxaca and Veracruz.

Huitlacoche: This difficult-to-pronounce, hard-to-find mushroom-like corn fungus is actually quite common. Wherever corn is grown, farmers battle this invasive field disease. A delicacy of Mexican haute cuisine, huitlacoche is seldom found in markets in the United States (see Mail-order Sources).

New Mexico red chile powder: This bright red, sweet, hot powder is made from whole ground chiles. Don't confuse it with the blended chili powders used for making chili con carne.

Nopal: The flat "leaf" or paddle of the nopal cactus, also known as the prickly pear cactus, is widely eaten in Mexico. Generally sold with the spines already removed.

Oaxacan string cheese: A mildly acidic string cheese.

Olive oil: For Mexican cooking, use the lighter tasting, neutral pure olive oils, as their more delicate flavor harmonizes best with the character of the fare.

Piloncillo: Cones of dark brown raw sugar.

Pork lard: The commercial pork lard found in most supermarkets is so refined that it has little flavor. Seek out freshly rendered pork lard in Mexican and Chinese markets, or flavor packaged pork lard with a few tablespoons of bacon drippings. You can also substitute olive oil for lard, but the authentic flavor will be sacrificed.

Queso fresco: A slightly tangy fresh cheese made from the strained, salted curds of cow's milk. I find it is similar to feta.

Tomatillos: Tomatillos are bright green to yellowish members of the gooseberry family. Like other gooseberries, they have a papery outer husk that must be peeled off before they can be used.

Tortillas: The corn tortilla not only finds a central place in every meal, but also defines dishes like quesadillas, tacos, and, in one form or another, most of those items that Mexicans call *antojitos*.

To make your own corn tortillas at home, see page 114. If making your own tortillas is not possible, don't despair. Commercial corn tortillas also can be very good. Look for the whitest ones (which indicates less lime was used in processing the corn and, hence, a more delicate flavor), and make sure they are fresh. Buy tortillas, just like bread, from a source that sells a lot of them. They should be very soft and flexible and, just like bread, eaten the day they are made.

To reheat tortillas, place them, one at a time, on a griddle or iron skillet preheated until very hot over medium-high heat and warm on each side until they color slightly. As they are warmed, stack and wrap them in a cotton towel and keep them wrapped until you are ready to use them. If you wish, the towel may be wrapped in foil and the packet kept in a 150°F oven for up to an hour to keep the tortillas warm. Tortillas may also be heated directly on the grates of a charcoal grill. The procedure is the same and they pick up a nice smoky flavor, although they are prone to burning.

Unseasoned Japanese rice wine vinegar: This neutral vinegar gives a perfect, if inauthentic jolt of acidity to Mexican dishes.

Tlayudas with Cheese

Basic Techniques

Making bocaditos is easy and fun. Some recipes may seem a bit involved, but nowhere is there the demanding sort of technique that experienced bakers or sauce makers are accustomed to. Remember, keep it simple and enjoy yourself. And when you come upon a technique in the recipe you're not sure about, you'll find the answer here.

Toasting herbs and spices: Toasting adds another layer of complexity to the taste of the herbs and spices. Generally, a recipe calls for only a small amount of an herb or spice; so toast a little extra, then you can have it around for the next time you need it. To toast the spice or herb, place it in a small, heavy, dry skillet over medium heat and heat just until fragrant and beginning to brown, usually less than 2 minutes. Transfer to a small bowl to cool, grind in a spice mill, and store in a tightly sealed jar.

Pan-roasting white onions, garlic, tomatoes, sweet peppers, and fresh and dried chiles: Pan-roasting ingredients on a dry *comal*, griddle or any flat, heavy pan adds a toasty, nutty flavor and is the secret to many of the complex flavors in *recados* and salsas. Heat the *comal* or pan over low or medium-low heat and arrange the vegetables on it without any added fats or oils. Cook carefully so they brown slowly but do not burn, and turn them occasionally to ensure that they cook evenly on all sides. When done, the vegetables will often "boil," that is, bubbles of water will be visible breaking through to the surface.

To pan-roast white onions, peel them and cut horizontally into ½-inch-thick slices. To pan-roast garlic, separate the heads into cloves, but do not peel until after cooking. Onions and garlic will take 10 to 20 minutes to cook. Leave tomatoes and tomatillos whole and unpeeled when pan-roasting, but remove the husks of the tomatillos. The tomato and tomatillo skins will blister and turn a deep brown where they touch the griddle. The same is true of sweet peppers and fresh chiles that are pan-roasted whole. Tomatoes, tomatillos, sweet peppers, and chiles are usually not peeled after pan-roasting—unless the skin is tough or charred—so try not to burn them. Pull off the stems and remove the seed cores (do not seed the peppers and chiles unless directed in a recipe) after they are pan-roasted. All of these may take a bit longer to roast than onions or garlic, depending on their size. Dried chiles can also be pan-roasted. Press them lightly against the griddle with a spatula; they will take only a few seconds to puff and become fragrant.

Frying dried chiles: This technique arrived with the Spanish; prior to that, the use of fat in cooking was not customary. The resulting chile flavor is slightly hotter than it would be if the pepper were toasted on a *comal* because capsaicim (the compound responsible for chiles' heat) dissolves in oil. To fry the dried chiles, place a small sauté pan over medium-high heat and add about 2 tablespoons corn oil. When it is hot, add the chiles and fry just until they puff and brown, 5 to 10 seconds. Do not let them burn or they will taste bitter. It is usually not necessary to drain the peppers on paper towels; simply shake off the excess oil. After frying, the chiles are often soaked in boiling water until soft, about 20 minutes.

Seeding and deveining dried chiles: Seeding and deveining chiles reduces their heat and alters their flavor. It is not always necessary to remove the seeds and stems, but if the recipe calls for it, begin by pulling off and discarding the stems. Break the chiles open, shake out the seeds, and then pull off the veins. They are now ready to be soaked, toasted, fried, or ground, depending on the recipe.

Handling and seeding fresh sweet peppers and chiles: If you have sensitive skin, wear plastic or rubber gloves when handling fresh chiles, as their natural oils can irritate and burn. Always wash your hands well immediately after you have finished working with chiles, and never touch sensitive parts of your body such as lips and eyes until you have done so.

Sometimes the instructions will say "remove the seed core," which means to pull off the stem. The fat central

Shrimp and Blue Corn Tamales Colados

seed core will come with it. Do not then remove the rest of the seeds, but slice or dice the chile as the recipe indicates. When the recipe says to seed the pepper or chile, pull off the stem and remove the seed core, then cut in half and cut out the white veins and shake out any remaining seeds.

Peeling fresh sweet peppers and chiles: The skins of sweet and hot peppers, especially of sweet bell peppers, can sometimes be tough. If this is the case, pull off the stem and remove the seed core. Cut the peppers lengthwise into pieces between the lobes. Cut out the veins, shake out the remaining seeds, and then use a sharp, swivel-bladed vegetable peeler to shave off the outer skin of the pepper.

Another technique that I prefer lessens the watery flavor and intensifies the color of sweet peppers, as they are much prettier raw than cooked in salads and salsas. After cleaning them, lay the pieces on a counter, skin side down, and press as flat as possible. Then, with a sharp paring knife, fillet the pieces, cutting off all the inside ridges and veins to leave only the fattest, most colorful flesh.

Roasting fresh sweet peppers and chiles: Select peppers and chiles with thick flesh and roast them over an open flame on the grill, in the fireplace, under the broiler, or over the flame of a gas burner. Turn the peppers so they blister and darken evenly. Put in a bowl, uncovered, and let steam several minutes until cool enough to handle. Pull off the stems and seed cores, and then peel off the skin if it is tough and/or burned; otherwise, don't bother. Cut out the veins and remove the seeds if you wish or if the recipe includes this step.

Roasting corn: Place the corn in its husk directly on the rack of a 500°F oven and roast for about 5 minutes. Remove and let cool. Shuck the corn and brush the ears with olive oil. Grill or broil the corn, turning as needed, until caramel brown all over, about 5 minutes.

Necessary Equipment

Comals, **griddles, and skillets:** The perfect tool for pan-roasting and toasting ingredients is the Mexican earthenware *comal*. Unfortunately these not only break easily, but are also hard to find in the United States. An old-fashioned cast-iron griddle, oval or round, is the perfect substitute. They are readily available and inexpensive. If you do not own one of these, however, a heavy-bottomed skillet or sauté pan is suitable for pan-roasting.

Molcajete: This lava-rock mortar is not only the best tool for making guacamole and many salsas, but it also makes a handsome serving dish. And it is easier to clean than a food processor.

Spice mill: The flavor imparted by freshly ground herbs and spices is one of the simplest, easiest ways for your home cooking to take a leap forward in quality. Buy a pepper mill for freshly ground pepper and an inexpensive electric coffee mill to devote to spices. You will find yourself using your spice mill often— for cumin seeds, for dried Mexican oregano, for dried chiles. Be sure to wipe well with a paper towel between uses.

Tongs: Long-handled, professional-style tongs are essential to successful grilling. They are inexpensive and permit you to pick up, move, and turn food easily on the charcoal grill, without tearing or piercing it.

Pork Rib Carnitas

botanas

The following recipes are perfect when you want to nibble on something spicy. A *botana* is, literally, a "plug" or "stopper."

It is meant to plug up that hunger you get at snack time, cocktail hour, or any time a little bite of Mexico fills your noshing needs. Included in this section are spicy-hot pumpkin seeds, delicate fried squash blossoms, an unusual and rich recipe for pork rib *carnitas*, three different small stuffed chiles, and much more. Try setting out a selection of *botanas* at your next party. They make for a perfect grazing meal.

Spicy Pumpkin Seeds

WHEN I'M HOMESICK FOR MEXICO I MAKE A BATCH OF THESE, FIX MYSELF A TALL, COLD *AÑEJO* AND SODA, AND SIT BACK WITH MY EYES HALF CLOSED. I FEEL LIKE I'M ALREADY BACK IN MEXICO. IF YOU CAN'T FIND THESE BRIGHT GREEN, HUSKED PUMPKIN SEEDS AT YOUR MEXICAN GROCER OR HEALTH-FOOD STORE, THIS IS GREAT MADE WITH SKIN-ON RED PEANUTS, TOO.

8 ounces hulled green pumpkin seeds
8 cloves garlic, unpeeled
1 tablespoon pequin chiles, or more to taste
2 tablespoons olive oil
¼ teaspoon salt
lime wedges

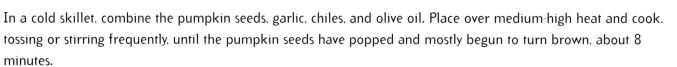

botanas

In a cold skillet, combine the pumpkin seeds, garlic, chiles, and olive oil. Place over medium-high heat and cook, tossing or stirring frequently, until the pumpkin seeds have popped and mostly begun to turn brown, about 8 minutes.

Using a slotted spoon, drain on paper towels and then place in a bowl. Toss with the salt and serve warm or at room temperature with lime wedges. They will keep a week or more in a tightly sealed container at room temperature.

Makes about 4 cups.

Ancho Chiles with Goat Cheese

ONE OF MY FAVORITE WAYS TO ENJOY THE DISTINC-
TIVE FLAVOR OF EACH OF THE MANY DIFFERENT
KINDS OF CHILES IS TO STUFF THEM. HERE, THE
DRIED-PLUM RICHNESS OF THE MILD ANCHO CHILE
PAIRS WITH GOAT CHEESE IN A WAY THAT REMINDS
ME OF SUN-DRIED TOMATOES AND GOAT CHEESE, A
COMBINATION POPULAR AT MY RESTAURANT LULU.

4 ancho chiles

8 ounces fresh goat cheese

2 cloves garlic, pan-roasted until browned and soft, then
  peeled

2 teaspoons fresh marjoram leaves, chopped

2 tablespoons plus ¼ cup olive oil

1 tablespoon freshly squeezed lime juice

1 tablespoon sherry vinegar

1 shallot, minced

grilled onion rings for garnish (optional)

Make a lengthwise slit in each chile with a knife and remove the seeds, keeping the chile intact. Place the cheese, garlic, and marjoram in a food processor and process until puréed. Stuff the chiles with the cheese mixture.

Heat the 2 tablespoons oil in a skillet over medium-high heat. When hot but not smoking, add the stuffed chiles and fry briefly on each side until they soften and just begin to change color, 10 to 15 seconds. Using a slotted spatula, drain the chiles on paper towels.

Put the warm chiles in a small bowl. In another bowl, stir together the lime juice, vinegar, shallot, and ¼ cup oil to form a vinaigrette. Pour over the chiles. Let marinate at least 1 hour at room temperature or overnight in the refrigerator. Serve at room temperature with a little of the vinaigrette, garnished with onion rings (if desired).

Makes 4 stuffed chiles.

Achiote Shrimp Brochettes with Grilled Pineapple Salsa

THIS IS BEACH GRILL FOOD. GATHER SOME BRANCHES AND BUILD A SMALL FIRE. THREAD SOME SHRIMP ON A SKEWER, SLATHER A LITTLE ACHIOTE *RECADO* (WONDERFUL YUCATÁN SPICE PASTE) ON THEM, AND LAY THEM ON THE GRILL. YOU DON'T EVEN NEED A KITCHEN, JUST A BEACH TO PUT YOUR GRILL ON. (YOUR DECK WILL DO JUST FINE, TOO.) ENJOY WITH AN ICE COLD BEER.

For the achiote *recado*:
1-ounce piece achiote paste
¼ cup freshly squeezed orange juice
2 teaspoons freshly squeezed lemon juice

For the grilled pineapple salsa:
1 slice (¾ inch thick) peeled and cored pineapple
1 Anaheim chile
1 small habanero chile, or less to taste
1 slice (½ inch thick) white onion
1 teaspoon olive oil

1½ pounds shrimp

botanas

To make the *recado*, put all the ingredients in a food processor and process until free of lumps; you will have about ⅓ cup. (This mixture can be stored in a tightly covered container for up to 5 days.)

Light the grill.

To make the salsa, place the pineapple, chiles, onion slice, and oil in a bowl and toss. Grill until soft and richly browned on all sides, about 10 minutes. Pull off the tops of the chiles. Place the salsa ingredients in a food processor or blender and purée. Set aside.

In a bowl, toss together the shrimp and *recado* until the shrimp are evenly coated. Thread onto skewers. Grill, turning frequently, until crusty and deep brown, about 4 minutes. Serve with the salsa.
Serves 6.

Achiote Shrimp Brochettes with Grilled Pineapple Salsa

Güero Chiles with Tuna

GÜERO MEANS "BLONDE," WHICH IS ALSO THE
COLOR OF THESE SPICY, PALE YELLOW CHILES.
CHARRED AND STUFFED IN THIS TRADITIONAL RECIPE,
THEY MAKE EVEN CANNED TUNA TASTE EXOTIC.

8 güero chiles

1 can (6 ounces) olive oil–packed tuna (preferably Italian
  or Spanish), drained

2 tablespoons minced scallion

3 green olives, pitted and chopped

3 fresh epazote leaves, minced

2 tomatoes, pan-roasted until blistered, deeply browned,
  and soft

2 tablespoons olive oil

pinch of toasted and freshly ground cumin

pinch of dried Mexican oregano, toasted and freshly
  ground

pinch of salt

botanas

Grill or broil the chiles until they are blistered all over and then peel, leaving the stems intact. Make a lengthwise
slit in each chile with a knife and remove the seeds, keeping the chile intact.

In a bowl, combine the tuna, scallion, olives, and epazote. Chop 1 of the tomatoes and add it, along with
its juices, to the bowl; mix well. Stuff the chiles with the tuna mixture and place in a shallow dish. Cut up the
remaining tomato and place in a food processor with the oil, cumin, oregano, and salt. Purée until smooth.
Pour over the chiles and serve at room temperature.

Makes 8 stuffed chiles.

Chiles de Agua with Corn and Squash Blossoms

CHILES DE AGUA ARE EASILY FOUND IN THE MAR-
KETS OF OAXACA. ANAHEIMS ARE AN ACCEPTABLE
SUBSTITUTE READILY AVAILABLE IN THE UNITED
STATES. IF YOU CAN'T FIND SQUASH BLOSSOMS, USE
A LITTLE FINELY DICED ZUCCHINI INSTEAD.

4 chiles de agua or Anaheim chiles
2 tablespoons olive oil
1 small white onion, minced
10 squash blossoms, stamens removed
1 ear of corn, in its husk, roasted and the kernels cut off
4 fresh epazote leaves, minced
$\frac{1}{2}$ cup crumbled *queso fresco*
salt and freshly ground black pepper

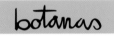 botanas

Grill or broil the chiles until they are blistered all over and then peel, leaving the stems intact. Make a lengthwise slit in each chile with a knife and remove the seeds, keeping the chile whole.

Heat 1 tablespoon of the oil in a skillet over high heat. When hot but not smoking, add the onion and sauté until limp. Add the squash blossoms, corn kernels, and epazote, and continue to sauté until the blossoms are wilted, about 2 minutes. Transfer to a bowl and let cool slightly, then add the *queso fresco* and mix well. Stuff the chiles with the blossom mixture.

Preheat a broiler. Brush the chiles with the remaining 1 tablespoon oil and sprinkle with salt and pepper. Broil until the cheese has melted, about 4 minutes. Serve hot or at room temperature.

Makes 4 stuffed chiles.

Pickled Vegetables with Chipotle

THESE PICKLES MAKE A WONDERFUL SNACK AT COCKTAIL TIME AND ARE EQUALLY APPRECIATED AS A RELISH IN SANDWICHES OR AS A SIDE DISH. YOU CAN CONTROL THE HEAT BY THE NUMBER OF SEEDS YOU LEAVE IN THE CHILES. YOU ARE BY NO MEANS LIMITED TO THE VEGETABLES LISTED HERE. SHOP FOR WHAT IS AT THE PEAK OF ITS SEASON. SERVE A BOWL OF THESE WITH MARGARITAS. YOU CAN HALVE THIS RECIPE IF YOU WANT, BUT SINCE PICKLES KEEP SO WELL, YOU MIGHT AS WELL MAKE A FULL BATCH.

4 cups apple cider vinegar

4 cups water

1 cup sugar

4 teaspoons salt

3 whole cloves

10 allspice berries

15 chipotle chiles, seeded and then fried in oil until puffed

5 baby fennel bulbs, quartered

2 bunches carrots with tops, peeled and cut into 2-inch lengths

10 small Yellow Finn potatoes, halved or quartered

4 red bell peppers, seeded, deveined, and cut into rings

5 small zucchini, cut in half lengthwise and then crosswise into 2-inch pieces

20 pearl onions, preferably red, peeled but left whole

20 cloves garlic, peeled but not crushed

1 head cauliflower, cut into florets

1 bunch fresh marjoram, chopped

¼ cup olive oil

botanas

In a large nonreactive pan, combine the vinegar, water, sugar, salt, cloves, and allspice. Cover and bring to a boil. Reduce the heat to low and simmer, covered, for 10 minutes. Add each vegetable, one at a time and in the order listed, beginning with the chiles and ending with the cauliflower. Cook each vegetable, covered, until it is just tender. The timing will depend on the particular vegetable: pierce with the tip of a sharp knife to check for doneness. Then, using a slotted spoon, lift out the vegetable, draining well, and spread it out on a baking sheet in a single layer to cool, either in the refrigerator or in front of a fan.

When all the vegetables have cooled, layer them in a large glass jar. Let the cooking liquid cool completely as well and add the marjoram and oil to it. Pour the liquid over the vegetables, cover tightly, and store in the refrigerator until ready to serve. The vegetables will keep for up to 2 weeks.

Makes about 1 gallon.

Oaxacan Pasilla Chiles with Picadillo

ONE OF MY FAVORITE OAXACAN BOCADITOS, THESE DELIGHTFUL *CHILES RELLENOS* ARE A PERFECT SNACK, MAIN COURSE, OR COMPONENT IN AN ELABORATE *BOTANA* PLATE, PERHAPS ACCOMPANIED WITH QUESADILLAS, *SOPES, QUESO OAXAQUEÑO* OR *QUESO FRESCO*, AND GUACAMOLE.

6 Oaxacan pasilla chiles or 9 chipotle chiles

1 cup boiling water

¾ cup Picadillo (page 108)

3 eggs

¼ teaspoon salt

3 tablespoons all-purpose flour

2 cups peanut oil for frying

Guacamole (optional; page 44)

botanas

Make a lengthwise slit in each chile with a knife and remove the seeds and veins. Place in a bowl and pour the boiling water over the top. Let soak for 1 hour.

Remove the chiles from the water, shaking off any excess. Stuff the chiles with the Picadillo and press to flatten slightly. Separate the eggs. Using a whisk, beat the whites with the salt until they stand in soft peaks. Lightly beat the yolks and fold them into the whites along with the flour. In a medium skillet over medium-high heat, preheat the oil to 325°F. Dip the chiles in the batter and slip into the oil. Fry each chile, turning once, until golden brown, about 2 minutes on each side. Using a slotted spatula, transfer to paper towels to drain. Serve warm or at room temperature, with the Guacamole, if desired.

Makes 6 or 9 stuffed chiles, depending on the chiles used.

Broiled Cheese with Pipián Verde

BROILED GOAT CHEESE TAKES ON A SLIGHTLY TANGY FLAVOR AND A MARVELOUS FLUFFY TEXTURE THAT COMPLEMENTS THE NUTTY RICHNESS OF THE DELICATE SALSA. THIS CONTEMPORARY DISH IS BOTH SUAVE AND RUSTIC.

8 ounces fresh goat cheese or *queso fresco*

½ cup Pipián Verde (page 97)

4 hot, fresh corn tortillas

Divide the goat cheese into 4 equal pieces and place in a single layer in a shallow flameproof baking dish. Pour some of the salsa around the goat cheese and broil until the top of the cheese browns slightly, about 5 minutes. Serve hot with corn tortillas.

Serves 4.

Broiled Cheese with Chipotle Chorizo

YOU CAN USE COMMERCIALLY PREPARED MEXICAN-STYLE CHORIZO, BUT IF YOU FEEL A LITTLE MORE ADVENTURESOME, MAKE THIS EASY CHORIZO. ITS SHARP SPICINESS TRANSFORMS BROILED CHEESE INTO A SMALL FEAT.

For the chorizo:
8 ounces coarsely ground pork shoulder
2 $\frac{1}{2}$ teaspoons dark Mexican beer such as Negra Modelo
2 teaspoons Chipotle Rub (page 103)

$\frac{1}{4}$ cup water
1 pound Oaxacan string cheese, shredded
6 fresh epazote leaves, chopped
4 to 6 hot, fresh corn tortillas

botanas

To make the chorizo, place the pork, beer, and chipotle rub in a bowl. Knead to mix well. Form into patties 3 inches in diameter. Cover and refrigerate for a few hours or overnight before using, to let the flavors develop. (It will not keep longer than 2 days.)

In a sauté pan over low heat, crumble the chorizo. Add the water and sauté until tender, about 30 minutes. Drain and set aside.

Preheat a broiler. In a bowl, stir together the cheese and epazote. Divide the mixture evenly among 4 small *cazuelas* (earthenware casseroles) or gratin dishes. Top with the chorizo. Broil until brown and bubbly, about 6 minutes. Serve immediately with hot corn tortillas.
Serves 4.

Broiled Cheese with Chipotle Chorizo

Albóndigas in Salsa Chipotle

These spicy little meatballs are among my favorite hors d'oeuvres for a party. Their flavor is traditional Mexican at its best. Try serving with rice or vermicelli as a main course, or even as a soup by adding 6 cups of broth to the recipe here.

For the meatballs:

1 tomato, pan-roasted until blistered, deeply browned, and soft, then chopped

1 white onion, finely chopped

2 cloves garlic

$\frac{1}{2}$ teaspoon freshly ground *canela*

$\frac{1}{2}$ teaspoon dried Mexican oregano, toasted and freshly ground

$\frac{1}{4}$ teaspoon black peppercorns, freshly ground

$\frac{1}{4}$ teaspoon allspice berries, freshly ground

1 tablespoon olive oil

2 tablespoons chopped green olives

2 tablespoons dried currants

1 tablespoon drained capers

8 ounces ground pork

8 ounces ground beef

$\frac{1}{4}$ cup fresh bread crumbs

2 eggs

$\frac{3}{4}$ teaspoon salt

botanas

For the salsa:

5 Oaxacan pasilla chiles or 4 chipotle chiles, seeded and then fried in oil until puffed

2 tomatillos, husked, rinsed, and pan-roasted until blistered, deeply browned, and soft

2 large tomatoes, pan-roasted until blistered, deeply
   browned, and soft
5 cloves garlic, pan-roasted until brown and soft, then
   peeled
$\frac{1}{2}$ teaspoon dried Mexican oregano, toasted and freshly
   ground
$1\frac{1}{2}$ cups chicken broth
1 teaspoon salt

To make the meatballs, in a sauté pan over medium heat, combine the tomato, onion, garlic, *canela*, oregano, black pepper, allspice, olive oil, olives, currants, and capers and sauté until the onion is soft, about 8 minutes. Transfer to a bowl and let cool. Add the pork, beef, bread crumbs, eggs, and salt to the onion mixture and knead together to mix well. Form into small meatballs about 1 inch in diameter.

In a nonstick pan over medium-high heat, sauté the meatballs, a few at a time, until they brown slightly on all sides, 4 to 5 minutes. Remove from the pan with a slotted spoon and set aside.

To make the salsa, place the chiles, tomatillos, tomatoes, garlic, oregano, chicken broth, and salt in a food processor and purée until smooth. Transfer the salsa to a large sauté pan and add the meatballs. Place over low heat, cover, and simmer very gently until the meatballs are cooked through, about 20 minutes. Serve at once or let cool, cover, and refrigerate for 3 to 4 days. Reheat gently just before serving.

Makes about 20 meatballs.

Wild Mushrooms in Salsa Verde

PEOPLE ARE OFTEN SURPRISED TO LEARN THAT WILD MUSHROOMS ARE PART OF MEXICO'S NATIVE CULINARY BOUNTY. THIS SIMPLE-TO-PREPARE DISH WORKS WELL WITH ANY KIND OF MUSHROOM, INCLUDING WHITE CULTIVATED ONES. SERVE IN SMALL BOWLS AS A *BOTANA* OR USE AS A GARNISH FOR SIMPLE GRILLED MEATS.

10 tomatillos, husked and rinsed

3 jalapeño chiles

1 clove garlic

8 fresh epazote leaves

¼ cup fresh cilantro sprigs

2 tablespoons olive oil

12 ounces fresh wild mushrooms, any kind, brushed clean

¼ teaspoon salt

3 tablespoons crumbled *queso fresco*

4 radishes, chopped

4 to 6 hot, fresh corn tortillas

botanas

Place the tomatillos, jalapeños, garlic, epazote, and cilantro in a food processor. Purée just until smooth. Set aside.

In a large skillet over medium-high heat, warm the oil. Add the mushrooms and sauté until they have begun to caramelize, about 4 minutes. Add the salt and sauté for 2 minutes longer. Add the tomatillo mixture and reduce over medium-high heat until the mushrooms are coated with the salsa.

Transfer to a bowl and let cool to room temperature. Sprinkle with the *queso fresco* and radishes and serve with the hot corn tortillas.

Serves 4.

Chicharrónes with Salsa Verde

CHICHARRÓNES ARE FRIED PORK SKINS. I KNOW THAT SOUNDS TERRIBLE. WHILE IT IS TRUE THEY ARE NOT EVERYDAY FOOD FROM A DIET STANDPOINT, THEY ARE ABSOLUTELY DELICIOUS. IN THIS TRADITIONAL RECIPE, THE CHICHARRÓNES ARE SIMMERED TO TENDERNESS IN A SPICY, HERBY BROTH. LITTLE BOWLS OF THIS SERVED WITH TORTILLAS MAKE A MARVELOUS BOTANA.

10 tomatillos, husked, rinsed, poached in water until soft, and drained

3 jalapeño chiles

1 clove garlic

8 fresh epazote leaves

$\frac{1}{4}$ cup plus 2 tablespoons chopped fresh cilantro

2 tablespoons olive oil

12 ounces *chicharrónes*

1 small white onion, finely diced

4 radishes, chopped

6 to 8 hot, fresh corn tortillas

 botanas

Place the tomatillos, jalapeños, garlic, epazote, and ¼ cup cilantro in a food processor and purée just until smooth to form a salsa. In a large skillet over medium-high heat, warm the oil and add the salsa. Cook, stirring, for 3 to 4 minutes. Lower the heat, add the *chicharrónes*, cover, and simmer until soft and tender, about 15 minutes.

Spoon into small *cazuelas* (earthenware casseroles) or gratin dishes and garnish with the onion, radishes, and 2 tablespoons cilantro. Serve with the corn tortillas.

Serves 4.

Pork Rib Carnitas

MANY PEOPLE KNOW *CARNITAS* AS THE BROWN, CRUSTY PIECES OF PORK THAT MAKE THE BEST TACOS AND BURRITOS. YOU CAN ALSO MAKE *CARNITAS* (LITTLE MEATS) OUT OF PORK RIBS. A SIDE OF RIBS COOKED THIS WAY COMES OUT CRUSTY, MOIST, AND FULL OF RICH FLAVOR.

1 side pork baby back ribs, about 1¼ pounds, cut into 3 pieces

3 tablespoons Chipotle Rub (page 103)

2 pounds pork lard or 4 cups olive oil

1 medium-sized white onion, thickly sliced (¾ inch), plus 1 small white onion, chopped

10 cloves garlic

2 tomatoes, chopped

2 jalapeño chiles, minced

1 tablespoon chopped fresh cilantro

salt

botanas

Place the pork ribs in a shallow nonreactive vessel and sprinkle the Chipotle Rub over them, coating evenly on all sides. Cover and refrigerate overnight.

The next day, in a heavy pan, melt the lard (or heat the oil) together with the sliced onion, garlic, and the ribs over medium-low heat. Slowly heat the ribs until they begin to sizzle, about 1 hour. Continue to cook until the ribs bubble and brown, about 30 minutes more.

In a bowl, stir together the chopped onion, tomatoes, jalapeños, cilantro, and salt to taste; set aside. Using tongs, remove the ribs from the cooking fat, draining well. Slice into individual ribs. Serve the ribs with the salsa. **Serves 4.**

Duck Carnitas

PORK IS NOT THE ONLY MEAT YOU CAN MAKE *CARNI-TAS* FROM. THE RICH FLAVOR AND FAT SKIN OF DUCK ARE TRANSFORMED INTO CRUSTY CHUNKS OF MOIST MEAT THAT ARE CLOSE TO HEAVEN. NIBBLE ON THESE BY THEMSELVES OR TUCKED INTO TORTILLAS AS TACOS.

6 duck legs

6 tablespoons Chipotle Rub (page 103)

2 pounds lard or olive oil

1 white onion, thickly sliced (¾ inch)

10 cloves garlic

1 cup Salsa Verde (page 95)

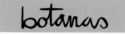

Arrange the duck legs in a shallow nonreactive vessel and sprinkle the Chipotle Rub over them, coating evenly. Cover and refrigerate overnight.

The next day, preheat an oven to 225°F. In a heavy ovenproof pan, melt the lard (or heat the oil) together with the onion, garlic, and the duck over medium-low heat on the stove top until warm. Then place in the oven and cook, uncovered, until tender, about 3 hours. Remove from the oven and let cool in the cooking fat.

To serve, remove the duck from the fat and place in a nonstick skillet over medium heat. Heat slowly, turning frequently, until well browned and crisp on both sides, about 8 minutes.

Transfer to a cutting board. When cool enough to handle, cut the meat from the bones and chop coarsely. Serve with the salsa.

Serves 4.

Guacamole with Chicharrónes

WHILE EVERYONE SEEMS TO HAVE THEIR OWN RECIPE FOR GUACAMOLE, THIS ONE IS MY FAVORITE. IT IS SIMPLE AND CAPTURES THE PURE FLAVOR OF THE AVOCADO. SO LEAVE OUT THE LIME JUICE, ONION, ETC. HERE, THE GUACAMOLE IS SERVED WITH CHICHARRÓNES, THAT DELICIOUS CRISP MEXICAN-STYLE FRIED PORK RIND, BUT IT IS ALSO GOOD WITH CHIPS OR AS A TOPPING FOR STUFFED CHILES AND OTHER BOCADITOS.

1 large avocado, pitted and peeled
¼ cup *queso fresco*
1 jalapeño chile, minced
pinch of salt
8 ounces chicharrónes, broken into large pieces

botanas

In a bowl, mash together the avocado, cheese, jalapeño, and salt. Serve with *chicharrónes*, to dip as you would tortilla chips.

Serves 4.

Guacamole with Chicharrónes

Fried Squash Blossoms

IF YOU ARE FORTUNATE TO LIVE IN AN AREA WITH A
GREAT FARMERS' MARKET OR IF YOU HAVE A GARDEN,
THE BEAUTIFUL YELLOW FLOWERS THAT GROW ON
ZUCCHINI WILL BE EASY TO COME BY. THEIR DELICATE
SQUASH FLAVOR AND VIBRANT COLOR MAKE THEM
WELL WORTH SEARCHING OUT. HERE, THEY FORM
THE WRAPPER FOR A SIMPLE STUFFING OF CHEESE,
CHILES, AND EPAZOTE.

8 large squash blossoms

8 pieces Oaxacan string cheese

8 small strips chile de agua or Anaheim chile

8 small pieces fresh epazote leaf

1 cup pastry flour

1 cup water

1 egg

¼ teaspoon salt

⅛ teaspoon cumin seeds, freshly ground

⅛ teaspoon coriander seeds, freshly ground

⅛ teaspoon freshly ground cayenne pepper

2 cups peanut or corn oil for frying

2 cups Pico de Gallo (page 99)

botanas

Remove the stamens from the squash blossoms. Stuff a piece of string cheese, a strip of chile, and a piece of epazote leaf inside each blossom. In a blender, combine the flour, water, egg, salt, and spices and blend until free of lumps. Let sit for 30 minutes to settle.

In a medium sauté pan, heat the oil to 350°F. One at a time, grab each blossom by the stem end, dip it in the batter, and then carefully lower it into the oil. Fry until light brown, 2 to 3 minutes. Using a slotted spoon, transfer to paper towels to drain. Serve hot with the salsa.

Makes 8 stuffed blossoms.

Grilled Corn with Huitlacoche Butter

THE EXOTIC-SOUNDING HUITLACOCHE IS A GRAY-BLACK "MUSHROOM" THAT GROWS INSIDE THE KERNELS OF CORN, CAUSING THEM TO SWELL. WHILE COMMONLY AVAILABLE IN MARKETS IN MEXICO, IT IS RARELY SEEN HERE, SINCE FARMERS DESTROY IT AS A PEST. IN THIS RECIPE, HUITLACOCHE FLAVORS A COMPOUND BUTTER SPREAD ON GRILLED CORN. I THINK YOU WILL FIND IT DELICIOUS. IF YOU CAN'T FIND HUITLACOCHE, SUBSTITUTE FRESH WILD MUSHROOMS OR TRY ORDERING IT THROUGH THE MAIL (SEE MAIL-ORDER SOURCES).

4 ears of corn, in their husks
3 tablespoons olive oil
4 ounces huitlacoche, morel mushrooms, or other
  wild mushrooms
salt
1 clove garlic, minced
1 jalapeño chile, minced
2 tablespoons finely minced white onion
4 fresh epazote leaves, minced
4 tablespoons (½ stick) unsalted butter, at room
  temperature
freshly ground black pepper

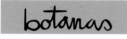 botanas

If you have very sweet corn, skip this step. If your corn is more mature or out of season, light the grill and lay the unshucked ears over the fire. Turn until the outsides of the ears are brown and charred, just a few minutes. Let the corn rest off of the heat for 10 minutes, then proceed with the recipe.

In a sauté pan over medium-high heat, warm 1 tablespoon of the oil. Add the huitlacoche (or mushrooms) and sauté until soft and lightly browned, 6 to 10 minutes. Add salt to taste, the garlic, jalapeño, onion, and epazote and sauté for 1 minute longer. Remove from the heat and let cool. Place in a food processor with the butter. Process until smooth, about 1 minute. Set aside.

Shuck the corn, rubbing off the silk with your hand or a towel. Brush the corn lightly with the remaining 2 tablespoons oil. Grill over a medium-hot fire, turning frequently, until the corn is a golden brown all over, about 6 minutes. Remove from the fire, sprinkle with salt and pepper and serve with the butter. Roll up your sleeves and enjoy. **Serves 1 to 4, depending on how good your corn is.**

Chalupas Poblanos with Shrimp and Nopales

antojitos

An *antojo* is literally a whim or a caprice. In this book, *antojitos* are "little whims" made from corn *masa,* the dough used to make tortillas. Here

we will venture from *enchiladitas* to *chalupas, sopes,*

tamales, and other flights of fancy.

Sopes are marvelous little corn *masa* "boats" that can be filled with almost any cargo of spicy, rich ingredients. A specialty of the town of Puebla, crisp, soft, oval *chalupas* can be topped with a nearly end-less variety of salsas and garnishes. *Enchiladitas,* little enchiladas filled with shrimp and avocado or corn and squash blossoms, make a terrific snack.

49

Wonderful *comal*-made quesadillas keep the delicacy of their fillings intact.

I have included recipes for two unusual types of tamales in this chapter,

one a barely cooked Zapotec tamale, the other a tamale from the Yucatán

made from a simmered *masa* akin to polenta.

All of these *antojitos* lend themselves to endless improvisation and

exploration. Enjoy them, as a whim.

Huaraches with Tomatillos and Crema

HUARACHES ARE SANDALS. THEY ARE ALSO THESE VAGUELY SANDAL-SHAPED *CHALUPAS* STUFFED WITH BEANS AND COOKED IN A TOMATILLO SAUCE. THESE DELICIOUS *BOTANAS* SHOWCASE THE VERSATILITY OF *MASA*. TRY THEM WITH DIFFERENT SALSAS, FILLINGS, AND GARNISHES.

1 pound *masa* for tortillas
1 cup Oaxacan Black Beans (page 110)
2 tablespoons olive oil
2½ cups Salsa Verde (page 95)
1 cup *crema*
fresh cilantro leaves

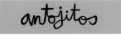

Divide the *masa* into 6 equal balls. Using a tortilla press or 2 large books, press the *masa* between two sheets of waxed paper to form ovals about ¼ inch thick. On top of 3 ovals, spread the beans in an even layer to within ½ inch of the edge. Top with the remaining ovals and press lightly around the edges to seal.

Preheat a *comal* or griddle over medium-high heat. Cook the *huaraches* on one side until they begin to brown, about 2 minutes, and then pour the oil evenly around them. Continue to cook, turning often, until browned and crispy on both sides, about 5 minutes more.

Pour the salsa into a 10-inch sauté pan and add the *huaraches*. Place over medium heat, cover, and simmer for 8 minutes. Meanwhile, in a small pan, warm the *crema*; do not allow to boil. Remove the sauté pan from the heat and divide between 3 plates. Pour the *crema* over the *huaraches*. Garnish with cilantro and serve.

Makes 3 *huaraches*.

Tlayudas with Cheese

These giant crispy tortillas are the base for a sort of Oaxacan "pizza," a simple snack food that is often just a combination of leftovers. The tlayudas themselves, the largest corn tortillas in Mexico, are a marvel of deft technique. In order to make a tortilla both so large and so thin, uncooked masa is scraped off of the tortilla right after it hits a hot griddle, leaving an almost crepelike disk. Try toasting other thin tortillas as outlined here. It is a simple way to make nutty-tasting tortilla chips without frying.

1 pound fresh corn *masa* for tortillas

1½ cups Oaxacan Black Beans (page 110), heated

1 nopal, cleaned, diced, cooked in boiling salted water for about 10 minutes until tender, and drained

4 ounces *queso fresco*

2 cups Pico de Gallo (page 99)

antojitos

Divide the *masa* into 3 equal balls. Place each ball in the center of a sheet of waxed paper 12 inches square and top with a second sheet. Using a book or piece of wood at least 12 inches square, press the tortilla flat. Press down hard, compressing the *masa* so that it is as thin as possible. With a rolling pin, finish rolling out the dough until you have a round approximately 10 inches or more in diameter.

Preheat a *comal*, large griddle, or cast-iron skillet over medium heat. Remove the top layer of waxed paper and invert the tortilla onto the heated surface. Remove the bottom sheet. Cook for 1 minute. Then, using a putty knife or similar wide, short-bladed knife, scrape the top layer of still-uncooked *masa* away, leaving a very thin and even tortilla. When the top begins to look dry, about 3 minutes, turn the tortilla over. Cook briefly on the second side until the tortilla has begun to color. Now, turning the tortilla every minute or two, continue to cook until the tortilla completely dries out and crisps, 3 to 5 minutes longer.

Repeat with the remaining *masa;* you should have 3 tortillas in all. To serve, spread each tortilla with the black beans and sprinkle with the nopal and *queso fresco.* Cut each tortilla into two pieces and serve with the salsa. Eat with knife and fork or your hands as you please.

Serves 6.

Duck Flautas with Pipián Verde

DUCK WITH GREEN PUMPKIN SEED SAUCE IS ANOTHER CLASSIC IN THE MEXICAN REPERTOIRE. IN THIS BOCA-DITO, I HAVE TAKEN LEFTOVER DUCK *CARNITAS*, CHUNKS OF SWEET POTATO, AND SWEET POTATO TORTILLAS AND ROLLED THEM UP INTO *FLAUTAS*. TOPPED WITH *PIPIÁN VERDE*, THEY ARE A SOPHISTI-CATED TREAT.

1 small sweet potato, peeled and cut into ½-inch chunks
1 tablespoon unsalted butter, melted
¼ teaspoon salt
¼ cup water
1 cup Duck Carnitas (page 43)
8 Sweet Potato Tortillas (page 112)
1 egg, beaten
2 cups peanut oil for frying
2 cups Pipián Verde (page 97), heated
4 radishes, sliced

antojitos

Preheat an oven to 450°F. Toss together the sweet potato chunks, butter, and salt in a small, heavy baking dish. Pour the water over top and roast until the water evaporates and the sweet potatoes are cooked through, about 35 minutes. Remove from the oven and transfer to a bowl; let cool.

Add the duck to the sweet potatoes and mix well. Put 3 tablespoons of the duck mixture on each tortilla and roll them up like rolling a cigarette. At the seam, brush the inside edge with a little of the beaten egg and press to seal. Skewer each *flauta* with a toothpick. Cover and refrigerate until needed (or up to 24 hours).

In a medium sauté pan, heat the oil to 330°F. Slip the *flautas*, a few at a time, into the hot oil and fry until golden brown and crisp, about 5 minutes. Using a slotted spoon, transfer to a clean towel to drain. Keep warm.

Place 2 *flautas* on each of 4 small plates and pour the hot sauce over them. Layer the radishes over the top and serve.

Serves 4.

Sweet Potato Flautas with Ancho Chile Sauce

SWEET POTATOES AND A RICH SAUCE OF MILD ANCHO CHILES FORM A PERFECT MARRIAGE IN THIS CONTEMPORARY DISH. YOU CAN MAKE IT WITH CORN TORTILLAS, BUT IT IS EVEN BETTER WITH SWEET POTATO TORTILLAS.

2 large sweet potatoes

2 tablespoons unsalted butter

2 tablespoons grated *piloncillo* or brown sugar

¼ teaspoon salt

dough for Sweet Potato Tortillas (page 112)

1 egg, beaten

½ cup fresh bread crumbs

2 cups peanut oil for frying

2 cups Ancho Chile Sauce (page 102)

toasted sesame seeds

antojitos

Preheat an oven to 400°F. Place the sweet potatoes directly on the oven rack and bake until soft throughout when pierced with a fork, about 45 minutes. Remove from the oven, prick, and let cool. Cut in half and scoop out the flesh from the skins into a bowl. Add the butter, *piloncillo* or brown sugar, and salt, and mix well.

Make the tortilla dough and roll out as directed. Cut the dough into 5-inch squares. Put 3 tablespoons of the sweet potato mixture on each square and roll them up like rolling a cigarette. At the seam, brush the inside edge with a little of the beaten egg and press to seal. Skewer each *flauta* with a toothpick. Dip each end of the *flauta* in the remaining beaten egg and then in the bread crumbs. Cover and refrigerate until needed (up to 24 hours).

In a medium sauté pan, heat the oil to 330°F. Slip the *flautas*, a few at a time, into the oil and fry until golden brown and crisp, about 5 minutes. Using a slotted spoon, transfer to paper towels to drain. Keep warm.

Place 2 *flautas* on each of 4 small plates and pour the hot sauce over them. Sprinkle with the sesame seeds and serve.

Serves 4.

Taquitos with Mole Rojo and Queso Fresco

THESE SIMPLE LITTLE FRIED TACOS ARE ONE OF MY
FAVORITE BOCADITOS. THE SPICY, RICH *PICADILLO*
PROVIDES A PERFECT BALANCE TO THE CRISP TOR-
TILLAS AND SPICY, SWEET *MOLE ROJO.*

1½ cups Picadillo (page 108)
8 small (4-inch) corn tortillas
2 cups peanut oil for frying
2 cups Mole Rojo (page 104), heated
3 ounces *queso fresco*

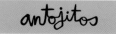

Place 3 tablespoons of the Picadillo inside each tortilla and roll them up like rolling a cigarette. Skewer each one with a toothpick. In a medium sauté pan, heat the oil to 330°F. Slip the rolled tortillas, a few at a time, into the hot oil and fry until golden brown and crisp, about 6 minutes. Using a slotted spoon, transfer to paper towels to drain. Keep warm.

Place 2 *taquitos* on each of 4 small plates and pour the hot *mole* over them. Crumble the cheese over the *mole* and serve.
Serves 4.

Taquitos with Mole Rojo and Queso Fresco

Sopes with Picadillo and Avocado

Spicy *picadillo* and creamy avocado make a traditional *bocadito*. The almost Moorish flavors of *picadillo* are one of the surprises of Oaxacan cooking.

1 pound Masa for Sopes (page 111)
¼ cup water
¾ cup Picadillo (page 108), heated
1 small avocado, pitted, peeled, and cut into thin slices
1 small white onion, diced
diced radish
queso fresco
fresh cilantro leaves

 .... antojitos

Divide the *masa* into 6 equal balls. Using a tortilla press or 2 large books, press the *masa* out between 2 sheets of waxed paper to form disks about ⅓ inch thick.

Preheat a *comal* or griddle over medium-high heat. Cook the *sopes* on one side until they brown slightly. Turn over, cook briefly until they change color, about 2 minutes more, and remove from the heat. With the browned side up, pinch up the sides of each *sope* to form a shell to hold the filling. Shape all of the rounds in the same way, then put the formed *sopes* back on the heated surface, flat side down, and cook over medium heat until cooked through, about 10 minutes.

To finish the *sopes*, put 2 tablespoons of the Picadillo inside each *sope*. Garnish with the avocado slices, onion, radish, *queso fresco*, and cilantro and serve.

Makes 6 *sopes*.

Sopes with Mushroom and Chipotle Chiles

SPICY WOODSY MUSHROOMS ARE LAYERED WITH TART CRÈME FRAICHE AND THE INTENSE SMOKY HEAT OF *CHILE CHIPOTLES EN ADOBO* TO MAKE THIS EXCITING BOCADITO.

1 pound Masa for Sopes (page 111)
¾ cup Wild Mushrooms in Salsa Verde (page 40), heated
6 tablespoons *crema*
2 *chiles chipotles en adobo,* drained and cut into strips
fresh cilantro leaves

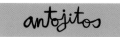

Divide the *masa* into 6 equal balls. Using a tortilla press or 2 large books, press the *masa* out between 2 sheets of waxed paper to form disks about ⅓ inch thick.

Preheat a *comal* or griddle over medium-high heat. Cook the *sopes* on one side until they brown slightly. Turn over, cook briefly until they change color, about 2 more minutes, and remove from the heat. With the browned side up, pinch up the sides of each *sope* to form a shell to hold the mushroom mixture. Shape all of the rounds in the same way, then put the formed *sopes* back on the heated surface, flat side down, and cook over medium heat until cooked through, about 10 minutes.

To finish the *sopes,* put 2 tablespoons of the mushroom mixture inside each *sope*. Top each with 1 tablespoon of *crema* and garnish with 1 or 2 strips of the chipotle chiles and cilantro and serve.

Makes 6 *sopes*.

Chalupas Poblanos with Roasted Wild Mushrooms and Goat Cheese

ROASTING INTENSIFIES THE SAVOR OF ANY KIND OF MUSHROOM, PLUS IT GIVES THE IRREGULAR EDGES OF WILD MUSHROOMS A PLEASANT CRISPNESS. THIS *CHALUPA* MAY NOT BE QUITE TRADITIONAL, BUT ITS FLAVOR IS PURE PUEBLA—INTENSE AND UNEXPECTEDLY SUAVE.

8 ounces wild mushrooms

1 tablespoon plus 4 teaspoons olive oil

1 clove garlic, chopped

1 serrano chile, chopped

3 fresh epazote leaves, chopped

¼ teaspoon salt

1 pound Masa for Sopes (page 111)

1 cup Salsa Verde (page 95)

4 ounces fresh goat cheese

antojitos

Preheat an oven to 500°F. In a bowl, toss together the mushrooms, 1 tablespoon oil, garlic, serrano, epazote, and salt. Spread on a baking sheet and roast until browned and crusty around the edges, about 10 minutes. Remove from the oven and set aside.

Divide the *masa* into 4 equal balls. Using a tortilla press or 2 large books, press the *masa* out between 2 sheets of waxed paper to form ovals about ⅓ inch thick.

Preheat a *comal* or griddle over medium-high heat. Cook the *chalupas* on one side until they brown slightly. Turn over, cook briefly, and pour 1 teaspoon of oil around each oval. Continue to cook, turning often, until browned and crispy on both sides, about 6 minutes more.

While the *chalupas* are still on the griddle, top each with 2 tablespoons of the salsa, spreading it with the back of a spoon to cover the surface completely. Sprinkle with the mushrooms and crumble the goat cheese over the top. Serve hot straight from the griddle.

Makes 4 *chalupas*.

Chalupas Poblanos with Shrimp and Nopales

THE FLAT PADDLE OF THE NOPAL CACTUS IS WIDELY EATEN THROUGHOUT MEXICO. ITS GREEN-BEAN-LIKE FLAVOR MARRIES PERFECTLY WITH THE SLIGHTLY IODINE FLAVOR OF GULF SHRIMP. THE PINK SHRIMP AND GREEN NOPALES ARE BEAUTIFUL AGAINST THE RED BACKGROUND OF THE SALSA.

1 tablespoon plus 4 teaspoons olive oil

6 ounces peeled and deveined shrimp, cut in half lengthwise

½ cup cleaned and diced nopal, cooked in boiling salted water for about 10 minutes until tender and drained

1 clove garlic, minced

¼ teaspoon salt

1 pound Masa for Sopes (page 111)

½ cup Salsa Roja (page 94), puréed until smooth in a blender

antojitos

In a large sauté pan over medium-high heat, warm the 1 tablespoon oil. Add the shrimp, nopal, and garlic and sauté until the shrimp curl and change color, about 3 minutes. Remove from the heat, mix in the salt, and set aside.

Divide the *masa* into 4 equal balls. Using a tortilla press or 2 large books, press the *masa* out between 2 sheets of waxed paper to form ovals about ⅓ inch thick.

Preheat a *comal* or griddle over medium-high heat. Cook the *chalupas* on one side until they brown slightly. Turn over, cook briefly, and pour 1 teaspoon of oil around each oval. Continue to cook, turning often, until browned and crispy on both sides, about 6 minutes more.

While the *chalupas* are still on the griddle, top each with 2 tablespoons of the salsa, spreading it with the back of a spoon to cover the surface completely. Scatter the shrimp mixture over the salsa. Serve hot straight from the griddle.

Makes 4 *chalupas.*

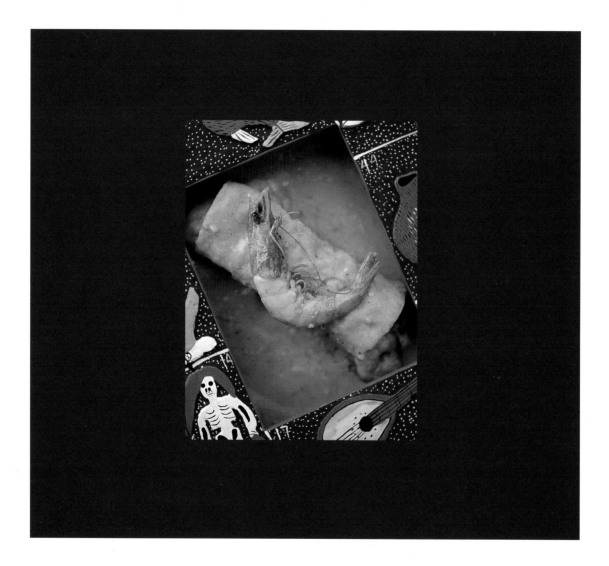

Shrimp and Avacado Enchiladitas

Shrimp and Avocado Enchiladitas

SHRIMP AND AVOCADO SEEM TO BE AMONG NEARLY EVERYONE'S FAVORITE FOODS. IN THESE SMOOTH, RICH-TASTING ENCHILADAS, THEY MATCH UP TO MAKE ONE OF THE BEST-SELLING DISHES AT CAFÉ MARIMBA.

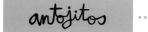

3 tablespoons olive oil

8 ounces shrimp, peeled, deveined, and coarsely chopped

1 clove garlic, chopped

3 fresh epazote leaves, chopped

¼ teaspoon salt

8 small (4-inch) corn tortillas

2 cups Taqueria Guacamole (page 101)

¼ cup *crema*

4 fresh cilantro sprigs

4 rings, cut from a small white onion

In a sauté pan over medium-high heat, warm 1 tablespoon of the oil. Add the shrimp, garlic, epazote, and salt and sauté until the shrimp change color, about 3 minutes. Remove from the heat and set aside.

In a nonstick pan over medium-high heat, warm the remaining 2 tablespoons oil and fry the tortillas, one at a time, until they begin to soften, about 15 seconds. Make sure they do not become crisp. Transfer them to paper towels to drain.

Meanwhile, warm the guacamole in a small pan. Dip the fried tortillas, one at a time, in the guacamole and top them with an equal amount of the shrimp filling. Roll them around the filling and then place 2 *enchiladitas* on each of 4 plates. Top with the remaining guacamole and drizzle with the *crema.* Garnish with the cilantro sprigs and the onion rings and serve.

Serves 4.

Corn and Squash Blossom Enchiladitas

THE DELICATE FLAVOR OF THE SUMMER GARDEN IS AT ITS BEST WHEN CONTRASTED WITH THE TART HOT *SALSA VERDE* AND THE CREAMY RICHNESS OF THE CHEESE IN THESE DELICIOUS *ENCHILADITAS.*

about 3 ears of corn
3 tablespoons olive oil
¼ cup diced white onion
3 fresh epazote leaves, chopped
¼ teaspoon salt
½ cup shredded squash blossoms
8 small (4-inch) corn tortillas
2 cups Salsa Verde (page 95)
½ cup crumbled *queso fresco*

antojitos

Remove the husks from the corn. Rub off the silks with your hands or a towel. Resting each ear upright in a bowl, cut the kernels from the cobs. As you work, cut about halfway through the kernels to expose their centers. Once you have cut all of the way around the cob, using the back of your knife, scrape out the creamy "milk" into the bowl. Measure the corn milk and kernels; you will need 1 cup.

In a sauté pan over medium-high heat, warm 1 tablespoon of oil. Add the corn, onion, epazote, and salt and sauté until the corn is heated through. Then add the squash blossoms and continue to sauté until they wilt, about 2 minutes. Remove from the heat and set aside.

In a nonstick pan over medium-high heat, warm the remaining 2 tablespoons oil and fry the tortillas, one at a time, until they begin to soften, about 15 seconds. Make sure they do not become crisp. Transfer them to paper towels to drain.

Meanwhile, warm the salsa in a small pan. Dip the tortillas, one at a time, in the salsa and top them with an equal amount of the corn filling. Roll them around the filling and then place 2 *enchiladitas* on each of 4 plates. Top with the remaining salsa, sprinkle with the *queso fresco,* and serve.

Serves 4.

Squash Blossom Quesadillas

THE DELICACY OF SQUASH FLOWERS IS CAPTURED NOWHERE AS PERFECTLY AS WHEN THEY ARE STEAMED INSIDE A QUESADILLA.

1 pound fresh corn *masa* for tortillas

8 ounces Muenster cheese, grated

12 squash blossoms, stamens removed and pulled into shreds

6 fresh epazote leaves

1½ cups Salsa El Topil (page 96)

Divide the *masa* into 6 equal balls. Using a tortilla press or 2 large books, press out the *masa* to form tortillas about ¼ inch thick. Preheat a *comal* or griddle over medium-high heat. Place 1 tortilla on the griddle. When it begins to color on the first side, after 2 to 3 minutes, turn it over and, working quickly, put one-sixth of the cheese, 2 of the squash blossoms, and 1 epazote leaf on the center. Fold the tortilla in half and press the edges together, sealing them lightly. Cook the quesadilla, turning frequently, until it is crisp all over and flecked with brownish black spots, 6 to 10 minutes. Repeat with the other tortillas, serving them as they come off of the fire.

Serve the quesadillas plain or with the salsa.

Makes 6 quesadillas.

Wild Mushroom Quesadillas

MUSHROOM QUESADILLAS ALWAYS SEEM TO BE A REAL FAVORITE. TRY THESE WITH MORELS WHEN THEY ARE IN SEASON.

1 pound fresh corn *masa* for tortillas

1 tablespoon olive oil

8 ounces wild mushrooms, any kind, brushed clean

1 clove garlic, pan-roasted until browned and soft, then peeled

1 chile poblano, roasted, peeled, seeded, and chopped

1 Roma tomato, pan-roasted until blistered, deeply browned and soft, then chopped with juice

¼ teaspoon salt

3 fresh epazote leaves, chopped

8 ounces Muenster cheese, grated

1 cup Roasted Corn Salsa (page 98)

antojitos

Divide the *masa* into 6 equal balls. Using a tortilla press or 2 large books, press out the *masa* to form tortillas about ¼ inch thick.

In a large sauté pan over medium-high heat, warm the oil. Add the mushrooms and garlic and sauté until the mushrooms soften and brown slightly, about 4 minutes. Add the poblano, tomato, and salt and simmer until the mushroom juices begin to evaporate, about 4 more minutes. Add the epazote, sauté for 1 minute, remove from the heat, and set aside.

Preheat a *comal* or griddle over medium-high heat. Place 1 tortilla on the griddle. When it begins to color on the first side, after 2 to 3 minutes, turn it over and, working quickly, put one-sixth of the cheese and one-sixth of the mushroom mixture in the center. Fold the tortilla in half and press the edges together, sealing them lightly. Cook the quesadilla, turning frequently, until it is crisp all over and flecked with brownish black spots, 6 to 10 minutes. Repeat with the other tortillas, serving them as they come off of the fire.

Serve the quesadillas with the salsa.

Makes 6 quesadillas.

Queso y Rajas Quesadillas

QUESO Y RAJAS MEANS CHEESE AND STRIPS OF CHILES. IN THIS VERSION, I USE BLAND STRING CHEESE FOR ITS TEXTURE AND STRIPS OF BRIEFLY FRIED CHIPOTLE CHILE FOR THEIR BITE. EPAZOTE GIVES ADDED DIMENSION TO THE OVERALL FLAVOR.

2 tablespoons olive oil

3 chipotle chiles, stemmed, seeded, and cut into strips (12 strips total)

1 pound fresh corn *masa* for tortillas

8 ounces string cheese, preferably Oaxacan, separated into thin, long strings

6 fresh epazote leaves

2½ cups Salsa Roja (optional; page 94)

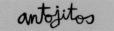

In a skillet over medium-high heat, warm the oil. When it is hot, fry the chiles, turning as needed, until they color slightly, 10 to 15 seconds. Using a slotted spoon, transfer to paper towels to drain. Set aside.

Divide the *masa* into 6 equal balls. Using a tortilla press or 2 large books, press out the *masa* to form tortillas about ¼ inch thick. Preheat a *comal* or griddle over medium-high heat. Place 1 tortilla on the griddle. When it begins to color on the first side, after 2 to 3 minutes, turn it over and, working quickly, put one-sixth of the cheese, 2 chile strips, and 1 epazote leaf in the center. Fold the tortilla in half and press the edges together, sealing them lightly. Cook the quesadilla, turning frequently, until it is crisp all over and flecked with brownish black spots, 6 to 10 minutes. Repeat with the other tortillas, serving them as they come off of the fire.

Serve the quesadillas plain or with the salsa.

Makes 6 quesadillas.

Huitlacoche Empanaditas with Salsa Roja

THE BLACK MUSHROOM-LIKE FUNGUS THAT GROWS ON CORN IS A DELICACY NOT SUFFICIENTLY APPRECIATED IN THE UNITED STATES. IF YOU CAN FIND HUITLACOCHE (SEE MAIL-ORDER SOURCES), TRY MAKING THESE DELICIOUS TURNOVERS. IF NOT, SUBSTITUTE WILD MUSHROOMS.

6 tablespoons olive oil

8 ounces huitlacoche, morel mushrooms, or other wild mushrooms

¾ teaspoon salt

1 jalapeño chile, minced

1 clove garlic, minced

2 tablespoons finely minced white onion

4 fresh epazote leaves, minced

1 pound fresh corn *masa* for tortillas

2 cups peanut oil for frying

1 cup Salsa Roja (page 94)

antojitos

In a sauté pan over medium-high heat, warm 2 tablespoons of the olive oil. Add the huitlacoche (or mushrooms) and sauté until soft and lightly browned, 6 to 10 minutes. Add ¼ teaspoon of the salt, the jalapeño, garlic, onion, and epazote and sauté for 1 minute longer. Remove from the heat and set aside.

In a large bowl, mix together the *masa* and the remaining 4 tablespoons olive oil and ½ teaspoon salt until you have a smooth paste. Divide into 8 equal balls. Using a tortilla or 2 large books, press the *masa* out between 2 sheets of waxed paper to form disks about ¼ inch thick. In the center of each round of *masa* place one-eighth of the huitlacoche mixture. Fold the round in half, covering the filling completely and forming a half-moon. Using your fingers, crimp the edges, rolling them over as well if you wish them to look like those of a pie shell.

In a deep sauté pan, preheat the peanut oil to 330°F. Add the *empanaditas*, two at a time, and fry until crisp and brown, about 6 minutes. Using a slotted spoon, transfer to paper towels to drain. Repeat with the remaining *empanaditas*. Serve hot with the salsa on the side.

Makes 8 *empanaditas*.

Huitlacoche Empanaditas with Salsa Roja

Mole Amarillo Tamales

Tamales like these are made by the Zapotec Indians near Oaxaca. Whether filled with fragrant *moles* or rustic black beans, these tamales are a surprise for their delicate texture and the brief time they cook. Unlike most tamales, these cook in under 8 minutes and maintain the fresh flavor of their filling. *Mole amarillo* is one of the easiest *moles* to make and is an exotic tribute to the depth of Oaxacan cooking.

1 pound plus 2 ounces fresh corn *masa*
12 large, fresh green corn husks, or 6 pieces banana leaf, each 10 by 8 inches
2 cups Mole Amarillo (page 106)
1½ cups shredded poached chicken breast meat
salt

 antojitos

Divide the *masa* into 6 equal balls. Using a tortilla press or 2 large books, press each ball between 2 sheets of waxed paper to form a tortilla about ¼ inch thick. Spread out 2 of the corn husks side by side, or lay out 1 piece of banana leaf. Peel off the top sheet of waxed paper and, using the bottom sheet, invert the *masa* round onto the pair of husks or the banana leaf. Peel off the second sheet of paper. Repeat with the other balls of *masa*.

In a saucepan over medium heat, combine the *mole* and chicken and heat just until warm. Taste for salt and then divide the mixture evenly among the tortillas, laying it in a strip down the center of the tortilla. Fold each edge of the tortilla over the *mole* mixture just to cover. You will end up with a package about 6 by 2 inches. Fold one long side of the husk over the filling and then the other. Fold the bottom up over the seam and fold the pointed end down. If using a banana leaf, fold in the long sides first and then fold over the ends to form a neat package.

Place the tamales seam side down on a steamer rack over boiling water, cover, and steam until the *masa* is cooked and easily separates from the wrapper, 6 to 8 minutes. Unwrap 1 tamale to test for doneness.

Serve the tamales immediately in their wrappers.

Makes 6 tamales.

Sweet Corn Tamales

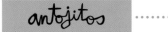

about 8 ears of corn, in their husks

1 tablespoon all-purpose flour

1 egg, separated

1 tablespoon minced white onion

¼ teaspoon salt

¼ teaspoon cumin seeds, toasted and freshly ground

1 poblano chile, roasted, peeled, seeded, and cut into 12 long strips

6 ounces Jack cheese, grated

1½ cups Salsa Verde (page 95) or Salsa El Topil (page 96)

Remove the husks from the corn, being careful not to tear them. Set the husks aside. Rub off the silks with your hands or a towel. Resting each ear upright in a bowl, cut the kernels from the cobs. As you work, cut about halfway through the kernels to expose their centers. Once you have cut all of the way around the cob, using the back of the knife, scrape out the creamy "milk" into the bowl. Measure the corn milk and kernels; you should have about 2 cups.

Sift the flour over the corn mixture and then stir into the corn, along with the egg yolk, onion, salt, and cumin. Whisk the egg white until soft peaks form and fold into the corn mixture.

Select 6 of the larger, softer husks to use as wrappers. Place them flat on a work surface. Divide the corn mixture evenly among them, placing it in a mound in the center. Then spread the mixture out into a 3-by-5-inch rectangle. Lay 2 poblano strips and one-sixth of the cheese on the center of each rectangle. Fold one long side of the husk over the filling and then the other. Fold the bottom up over the seam and then fold the pointed end down. Line a steamer rack with the extra corn husks and place the tamales, seam side down, on the rack. Place over boiling water, cover, and steam until cooked through, about 15 minutes.

Serve warm with Salsa Verde or Salsa El Topil.

Makes 8 tamales.

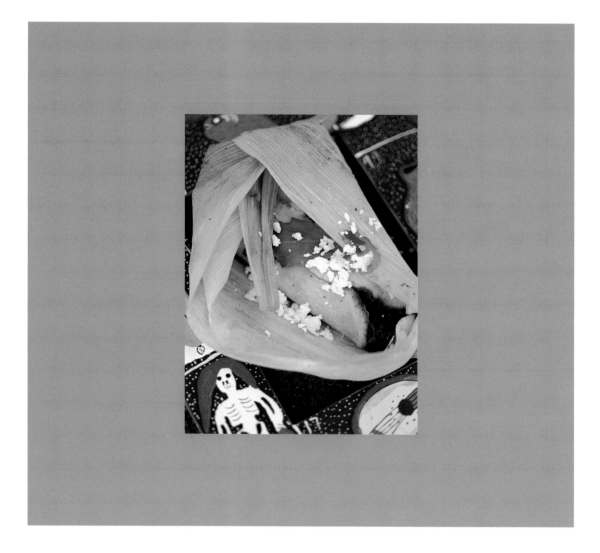

Black Bean Tamales

Black Bean Tamales

Black bean tamales are peasant food. But like many dishes created out of necessity, they are both delicious and a marvel of rustic simplicity.

1 pound plus 2 ounces fresh corn *masa*

12 large, fresh green corn husks, or 6 pieces banana leaf, each 10 by 8 inches

4 cups Oaxacan Black Beans (page 110)

2 tablespoons olive oil

Divide the *masa* into 6 equal balls. Using a tortilla press or 2 large books, press each ball between 2 sheets of waxed paper to form a disk about ¼ inch thick. Spread out 2 of the corn husks side by side, or lay out 1 piece of banana leaf. Peel off the top sheet of waxed paper and, using the bottom sheet, invert the *masa* round onto the pair of husks or the banana leaf. Peel off the second sheet of paper. Repeat with the other balls of *masa*.

Meanwhile, in a large nonstick skillet over medium heat, combine the black beans and oil. Cook, stirring often, until the beans have dried and become a thick paste, about 15 minutes. Remove from the heat and let cool slightly. Divide the mixture evenly among the tortillas, laying it in a strip down the center of each tortilla. Fold each edge of the tortilla over the beans just to cover. You will end up with a package about 6 by 2 inches. Fold one long side of the husk over the filling and then the other. Fold the bottom up over the seam and fold the pointed end down. If using a banana leaf, fold in the long sides first and then fold over the ends to form a neat package.

Place the tamales seam side down in a steamer rack over boiling water, cover, and steam until the *masa* is cooked and easily separates from the wrappers, 6 to 8 minutes. Unwrap 1 tamale to test for doneness.

Serve the tamales immediately in their wrappers.

Makes 6 tamales.

Shrimp and Blue Corn Tamales Colados

COLADO MEANS "STRAINED." IN THIS TAMALE, WHICH IS TRADITIONAL IN THE YUCATÁN, THE MASA IS MIXED WITH WATER, STRAINED TO REMOVE ITS GRIT, AND THEN COOKED LIKE POLENTA. HERE I FLAVOR THE MIXTURE WITH SHRIMP BUTTER AND STUFF IT WITH SAUTÉED SHRIMP. IF YOU CAN'T FIND BLUE CORN MASA, REGULAR FRESH CORN MASA WILL DO. THE BLUE CORN DOES HAVE A MORE DELICATE, SWEET FLAVOR, HOWEVER.

3 cups fresh corn *masa* for tortillas, preferably blue corn *masa*

8 ounces peeled and deveined shrimp, with shells (and heads, if possible) reserved

4 cups water

2 tablespoons olive oil

3 cloves garlic, pan-roasted until browned and soft, then peeled and chopped

1 large poblano chile, roasted, peeled, seeded, and diced

1/2 teaspoon fresh marjoram leaves, chopped

1/4 teaspoon salt

4 ounces (1 stick) unsalted butter

8 pieces banana leaf, each 10 by 8 inches

 antojitos

In a bowl, whisk together the *masa* and water, blending thoroughly. Strain the mixture through a medium-fine sieve placed over a bowl to remove any grit. Set aside.

In a large sauté pan over high heat, sauté the shrimp in the oil with the garlic and chiles, the marjoram, and the salt. Cook until the shrimp turn pink and stiffen, about 4 minutes. Remove from the heat and set aside.

Meanwhile, put the butter and shrimp shells (and heads, if available) in a food processor and process until thoroughly blended. Transfer to a small saucepan and heat gently over medium-low heat to melt the butter. Then continue to cook until the mixture boils. Immediately pour it through a medium-fine sieve, pressing hard with the back of a spoon to remove as much of the butter from the shells as possible.

Combine the *masa* mixture and shrimp butter in a heavy-bottomed saucepan and place over medium-high heat. Cook, stirring constantly, until the mixture thickens and boils, about 10 minutes. You should end up with something that looks like thick, smooth polenta.

Acting quickly, divide the mixture evenly among the banana leaves, spreading it out with the back of a spoon to make a rectangle about 4 by 6 inches on the center of each leaf. Divide the cooked shrimp among the 8 tamales, arranging them in a band lengthwise down the center. Fold each tamale over to seal in the filling. Fold in the long sides of each banana leaf first and then fold over the ends to form a neat package. At this point, the tamales may be covered and refrigerated for up to 24 hours.

Place the tamales on a steamer rack over boiling water, cover, and steam until the *masa* is cooked and easily separates from the wrappers, 6 to 10 minutes. Unwrap 1 tamale to test for doneness.

Serve the tamales immediately in their wrappers.

Makes 8 tamales.

Tuna Ceviche Verde

mariscos

Mariscos means "seafood." And I can think of no "little bite" I like better than fresh seafood. In

this chapter we try the full range of Mexican seafood bocaditos, from simple raw clams on the half shell with red chile and lime to spicy shrimp prepared with chipotle,

a traditional pick-me-up called *vuelve la vida,*

and an addictive sauté of crabs with garlic and lime. Put yourself in the beach frame of mind, cook up a selection of these delicious bocaditos, and

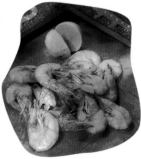

invite over a few friends. Dream of old Veracruz in the days of Carmen Miranda and Desi Arnaz.

Oysters with Pineapple Salsa

TRULY GREAT FRESHLY SHUCKED OYSTERS ARE ONLY
IMPROVED BY A SIMPLE, CLEAN-FLAVORED RELISH OR
SALSA. THIS IS ONE OF MY FAVORITE COMBINATIONS.

12 freshly shucked, plump oysters on the half shell
$^1/_2$ cup Pineapple Salsa (page 100)

mariscos

Top each oyster with a little bit of the salsa. Serve immediately.
Serves 2.

Shrimp en Chipotlada

This spicy little dish makes a great sort of Mexican tapa. It can be served hot or at room temperature. Try it with a cold beer.

mariscos

5 tablespoons olive oil

3 chipotle chiles, seeded and deveined

$\frac{1}{2}$ cup boiling water

1 tomato, pan-roasted until blistered, deeply browned, and soft

2 cloves garlic pan-roasted until browned and soft, then peeled

1 slice ($\frac{1}{2}$ inch thick) white onion, pan-roasted until browned and soft

$\frac{1}{2}$ teaspoon salt

1 pound shrimp with heads on

6 fresh epazote leaves

lime wedges

In a skillet over medium-high heat, warm 2 tablespoons of the oil. When it is hot, add the chiles and fry until puffed and browned, 5 to 10 seconds. Remove from the pan, shaking off the excess oil, and place in a bowl. Add the boiling water and let soak until soft, about 20 minutes. In a blender, combine the chiles and their soaking water, tomato, garlic, onion, and salt and purée until smooth. Set aside.

In a large skillet over medium-high heat, warm the remaining 3 tablespoons oil. Add the shrimp and sauté until they begin to turn pink. Add the purée and sauté until the shrimp are cooked through, about 2 minutes more.

Transfer to a bowl, add the epazote, and toss well. Serve hot or warm with lime wedges.

Serves 4.

Shrimp Boca del Rio

ON THE BEACH NEAR THE MOUTH OF THE VERACRUZ RIVER, YOUNG CHILDREN SELL FRESHLY CAUGHT SHRIMP, STILL WARM FROM A BRIEF COOKING IN SALTY GULF SEA WATER. THEY ARE SERVED ON NEWSPAPER WITH LIME WEDGES AND A FIERY SALSA MADE FROM *CHILES MORITAS*, A SORT OF CHIPOTLE. THIS IS ONLY IMPROVED BY GOOD COMPANY, A COLD RUM COCONUT, AND A SUNNY DAY.

For the Veracruz salsa:
12 morita chiles, or 8 chipotle chiles, fried in oil
    until puffed
2 cloves garlic, pan-roasted until browned and soft,
    then peeled
1 tomato, pan-roasted until blistered, deeply browned,
    and soft
1½ cups hot water
¼ teaspoon salt

4 quarts water
1 cup sea salt
2 cups fresh seaweed or 2 bunches fresh cilantro
2 pounds fresh shrimp with heads on (don't bother with
    frozen shrimp)
3 limes, cut into wedges

 Mariscos

To make the salsa, combine all the ingredients in a blender and blend until very smooth. You will have about 2 cups. The salsa can be used immediately or covered tightly and refrigerated for up to 2 days.

In a large pot, combine the water, sea salt, and seaweed (or cilantro) and bring to a boil. Reduce the heat to low, cover, and simmer for 5 minutes to blend the flavors. Add the shrimp and cook until they begin to turn pink and are just cooked through, 2 to 6 minutes, depending on their size. Drain the shrimp and spread out on a large platter. Do not refrigerate.

Serve while still warm with the lime wedges and salsa.

Serves 8.

Shrimp Boca del Rio

Ceviche Tostadas

Crispy tostadas are one of the best ways to enjoy ceviche. I like to make all different kinds of ceviche. This one uses cooked shrimp, crab, and squid.

3 cups water

1 bunch fresh cilantro

10 allspice berries

4 whole cloves

3 tablespoons sea salt

4 ounces peeled and deveined shrimp

4 ounces cleaned squid, tentacles left whole and tubes cut into rings

$\frac{1}{2}$ cup freshly squeezed lime juice

$\frac{1}{4}$ teaspoon salt

$\frac{1}{2}$ cup fresh cooked crab meat

1 avocado, pitted, peeled, and then cut into chunks

2 tomatoes, diced

$\frac{1}{2}$ habanero chile or 2 jalapeño chiles, diced

1 small sweet red onion, diced and rinsed first in hot water and then in cold water

2 tablespoons coarsely chopped fresh cilantro

4 radishes, diced

1 tablespoon olive oil

$\frac{1}{2}$ cup peanut oil

6 corn tortillas

$\frac{1}{2}$ cup mayonnaise

mariscos

In a saucepan, bring the water to a boil with the cilantro, allspice, cloves, and sea salt. Cover, reduce the heat to low, and simmer for 10 minutes.

Uncover the pan and, in the seasoned liquid, poach first the shrimp until pink, about 2 to 3 minutes, and then the squid until stiffened, about 30 seconds. Drain and let cool in a single layer on a plate in the refrigerator.

Combine the lime juice and salt in a glass or stainless-steel bowl. Add the crab and cooled shrimp and squid and mix well. Fold in the avocado, tomatoes, chiles, onion, cilantro, radishes, and olive oil.

In a medium sauté pan, heat the peanut oil to 330°F. Slip the tortillas, a few at a time, into the hot oil and fry until golden brown and crisp, about 3 to 4 minutes. Using a slotted spoon or tongs, transfer them to paper towels to drain. Keep warm.

Spread the mayonnaise on the warm tortillas, dividing it evenly. Top with the ceviche, again dividing evenly, and serve at once.

Makes 6 tostadas.

Tuna Ceviche Verde

THE FLAVOR OF RICH, OILY-FLESHED FISH SUCH AS TUNA, SIERRA, SARDINES, OR MACKEREL IS IDEAL FOR THE SHARP, BRIGHT TASTE OF THIS CEVICHE. WHENEVER YOU MAKE CEVICHE, BE SURE TO BUY YOUR FISH FROM A TRUSTED FISH MARKET. IT IS MORE IMPORTANT THAT THE FISH BE TRULY FRESH THAN WHAT KIND OF FISH YOU GET. ASK WHEN THE FISH WAS CAUGHT. MOST REPUTABLE MARKETS WILL KNOW AND BE HAPPY TO TELL YOU.

1 pound fresh tuna fillet or other rich, oily-fleshed fish fillets

2 cups freshly squeezed lime juice

1 tablespoon salt

2$\frac{1}{2}$ cups Salsa Verde made with 2 scallions (including green tops), minced, in place of the white onion (page 95)

1 avocado, pitted, peeled, and cut into chunks

2 fresh epazote leaves, minced

2 tablespoons olive oil

4 radishes, diced

tortilla chips

mariscos

Cut the fish into pieces 1$\frac{1}{2}$ inches long by $\frac{1}{2}$ inch wide by $\frac{1}{2}$ inch thick. Combine the lime juice and salt in a glass or stainless-steel bowl. Add the fish and refrigerate until the fish is just opaque throughout, about 2 hours.

Drain the fish well and discard the lime juice. Place in a bowl and add the salsa, mixing well. Fold in the avocado, epazote, oil, and radishes. Serve with tortilla chips.

Serves 4 to 6 people.

Clams with Red Chile and Lime

THIS RECIPE IS SIMPLICITY ITSELF. IF YOU LIVE ON THE EAST COAST OR SOMEWHERE WHERE YOU CAN GET GREAT FRESH CLAMS, YOU MUST TRY THIS. IT IS ONE OF THE VERY BEST *MARISCOS*.

**12 freshly shucked littleneck or Manila clams
  on the half shell
New Mexico red chile powder or ancho chile powder
  (but not the spice mix called chili powder)
3 limes, each cut into 4 wedges**

mariscos

Sprinkle each clam with a pinch of chile powder. Serve with the lime wedges and squeeze a bit of lime on each clam just before eating.

Serves 2.

Vuelve la Vida

VUELVE LA VIDA MEANS "TO RETURN TO LIFE." THIS IS THE TRADITIONAL HANGOVER CURE SERVED ON BEACHES IN MEXICO. ALMOST ANY KIND OF COOKED OR RAW SEAFOOD CAN BE USED. YOU SHOULD BE SURE AND INCLUDE SHUCKED OYSTERS, THOUGH.

mariscos

3 tomatoes
6 freshly shucked oysters with their liquor
2 ounces cleaned squid, tentacles left whole and tubes cut into rings, poached as in Ceviche Tostadas (page 82)
2 ounces peeled and deveined shrimp, poached as in Ceviche Tostadas (page 82)
2 ounces fresh cooked crab meat
4 ounces snapper fillet cured in 1 teaspoon salt and 2/3 cup freshly squeezed lime juice as in Tuna Ceviche Verde (page 84)
2 tablespoons diced sweet red onion, rinsed first in hot water and then in cold water
1 avocado, pitted, peeled, and diced
juice of 1 lime
2 jalapeño chiles, minced
dash of Worcestershire sauce
2 dashes of Tabasco sauce
1 tablespoon chopped fresh cilantro
lime wedges

Peel the tomatoes by plunging them in boiling water for 1 minute and then slipping off their skins. Cut the tomatoes in half and squeeze out their seeds and juice. Place in a food processor or blender and purée until smooth. Pour into a bowl and add all the remaining ingredients except the lime wedges. Divide the mixture between 2 sundae dishes. Garnish with lime wedges and serve.
Serves 2.

Vuelve la Vida

Crab Salpicón

SALPICÓN MEANS "A LITTLE BIT." WHEN YOU MAKE THIS DISH, YOU SHOULD MAKE MORE THAN JUST A LITTLE BIT. EVERYONE SEEMS TO LOVE CRAB, PARTICULARLY IN THIS FORM. BE SURE TO MAKE A LOT. IT GOES FAST.

1½ cups fresh cooked crab meat

2 scallions, including green tops, minced

1 red bell pepper, seeded, peeled (pages 20-22), and finely diced

1 yellow bell pepper, seeded, peeled (pages 20-22), and finely diced

1 small habanero chile, or to taste, finely diced

1 avocado, pitted, peeled, and diced

2 fresh mint leaves, minced, or 3 fresh epazote leaves, minced

10 fresh cilantro leaves, minced

2 tablespoons unseasoned Japanese rice wine vinegar

1 tablespoon freshly squeezed lime juice

3 tablespoons freshly squeezed orange juice

warm tortilla chips

Mariscos

Combine all the ingredients, except the chips, in a bowl and mix gently. Serve cold with warm tortilla chips.

Serves 4.

Crabs en Mojo de Ajo

A SPECIALTY OF MOCAMBO BEACH IN VERACRUZ.
WHEN YOU EAT THIS DISH HOT, THE GARLICKY CRAB
STICKS TO YOUR FINGERS. MAKE SURE YOU SERVE IT
WITH PLENTY OF NAPKINS AND COLD BEER.
DELICIOUS WITH SOFT SHELL CRABS.

6 blue crabs
2 tablespoons unsalted butter
2 tablespoons olive oil
10 cloves garlic, sliced
1 jalapeño chile, cut into rings
½ small white onion, cut into half-moons
¼ cup fresh parsley leaves
¼ teaspoon salt
4 fresh epazote leaves, chopped
juice of 2 limes

mariscos

Pull the backs off of the crabs and then cut the bodies in half. Pull out the gills and the stomach from each and discard.

In a sauté pan over medium heat, melt the butter with the oil. Add the crabs and garlic and sauté until the garlic begins to color. Add the jalapeño and onion, raise the heat to medium-high, and continue to sauté until the garlic is golden brown and fragrant, about 3 minutes more. Add the parsley, salt, and epazote and toss well. Mix in the lime juice and serve very hot.

Serves 4 to 6.

Pickled Crabs

I LOVE TO EAT CRAB IN THE SHELL. IT IS A LOT OF WORK, BUT IT IS GOOD WORK. THERE IS SOMETHING SATISFYING ABOUT PRYING OUT THE LITTLE BITS OF MEAT WITH A FORK. THESE PICKLED CRABS MAKE A TERRIFIC FIRST COURSE OR SNACK.

11 cups water

2 bunches fresh cilantro

20 allspice berries

6 whole cloves

6 tablespoons sea salt

1 head garlic, cut in half through stem end

3 pounds live blue crabs, or 1 large live Dungeness crab

4 cups unseasoned Japanese rice wine vinegar

$\frac{1}{2}$ cup sugar

2 teaspoons salt

1 cup freshly squeezed orange juice

$\frac{1}{4}$ cup freshly squeezed lime juice

1 habanero chile, minced

1 red bell pepper, seeded and peeled (pages 20-22),
   then finely diced

1 yellow bell pepper, seeded and peeled (pages 20-22),
   then finely diced

1 carrot, peeled and finely diced

2 shallots, finely diced

2 fresh mint leaves, minced

10 fresh cilantro leaves, minced

mariscos

In a large pot, combine 9 cups of the water, with the cilantro bunches, allspice, cloves, sea salt, and garlic. Reduce the heat to low, cover, and simmer for 10 minutes to blend the flavors. Add the blue crabs or Dungeness crab to the liquid and cook until done, about 5 minutes for the blue crabs and about 10 minutes for the Dungeness crab.

Scoop out the crab(s) from the liquid and, while still hot, pull off the back(s). Pull out the gills and the stomach(s) and discard. If using a Dungeness crab, cut the body into 8 pieces. Crack the claws and bodies and place in a large, clear glass bowl. In another bowl or a pitcher, mix together all the remaining ingredients with the remaining 2 cups of water, stirring to dissolve the sugar. Pour over the crab pieces to submerge completely. Cover and refrigerate, letting the crab(s) cool completely in the liquid, or for up to 5 days.

Serve the crab pieces directly from the bowl.

Serves 4 to 6.

Grilled Corn with Huitlacoche Butter

basics

Bocaditos are typically quickly made or readily assembled

snacks. These little bites depend

on the chef's familiarity with

certain basic recipes. While I do

not even begin to scratch the surface of salsas, *recados,*

moles, masas, and other preparations here, the following bag of

tricks is more than sufficient to assist the

reader in preparing

a much wider range of

bocaditos than outlined in this book.

Salsa Roja

THIS IS THE SALSA MOST PEOPLE THINK OF WHEN THEY THINK OF SALSA. RED, SPICY WITH JALAPEÑO, AND CHUNKY, IT GOES WITH ALMOST EVERY SAVORY FOOD.

2 large tomatoes, pan-roasted until blistered, deeply browned, and soft

3 jalapeño chiles, pan-roasted until blistered and deeply browned

1 small white onion, thickly sliced (³/₄ inch) and pan-roasted until browned and soft

2 cloves garlic, pan-roasted until browned and soft, then peeled

¼ teaspoon dried Mexican oregano, toasted and freshly ground

¼ teaspoon cumin seeds, toasted and freshly ground

½ cup water

salt

basics

Using a knife or food processor, chop together the tomatoes, chiles with seeds, onion, and garlic until you have a coarsely textured salsa. Add the oregano and cumin, thin with the water, and add salt to taste. Use immediately, or cover and refrigerate for up to 3 days. Bring to room temperature before serving.
Makes about 2¹/₂ cups.

Salsa Verde

THIS BRIGHT GREEN, SLIGHTLY ASTRINGENT SALSA IS
PERFECT WITH ALL RICH-FLAVORED FOODS.

basics ....

10 tomatillos, husked, rinsed, poached in water until
    soft, and drained
2 serrano chiles with seeds
$\frac{1}{4}$ cup coarsely chopped fresh cilantro
$\frac{1}{2}$ cup water
$\frac{1}{4}$ teaspoon salt
$\frac{1}{4}$ cup finely diced white onion

Place all the ingredients except the onion in a blender or food processor and purée until smooth. Fold in the
onion. This salsa is best the day it's made.
Makes about 2$\frac{1}{2}$ cups.

Salsa El Topil

THIS SALSA IS FREQUENTLY ON THE TABLE OF EL TOPIL, MY FRIEND SOLEDAD'S WONDERFUL RESTAURANT IN OAXACA. THE SMOKY, RICH FLAVOR OF THE OAXACAN PASILLA CHILES IS EXQUISITE. THESE CHILES ARE HAND ROLLED IN HOT EMBERS TO FACILITATE DRYING. IF YOU AREN'T GOING TO OAXACA SOON, THE CHILES ARE AVAILABLE BY MAIL FROM CAFÉ MARIMBA (SEE MAIL-ORDER SOURCES). IF YOU DO MAKE IT TO OAXACA, STOP BY EL TOPIL AND SAY HELLO TO SOLEDAD.

3 pasilla chiles, preferably Oaxacan variety, with seeds

1 tomatillo, husked, rinsed, and pan-roasted until blistered, browned, and soft

1 large tomato, pan-roasted until blistered, deeply browned, and soft

3 cloves garlic, pan-roasted until browned and soft, then peeled

$\frac{1}{4}$ teaspoon dried Mexican oregano, toasted

$\frac{1}{4}$ teaspoon salt

$\frac{3}{4}$ cup water

basics

In a heavy skillet over medium heat, toast the chiles until browned and fragrant, about 3 minutes. Transfer to a blender and add all the remaining ingredients. Process at high speed until you have a coarsely textured liquid. It will keep, tightly covered, in the refrigerator for 2 to 3 days.

Makes about 1$\frac{1}{2}$ cups.

Pipián Verde

THIS GREEN PUMPKIN SEED SALSA IS REALLY A SORT OF *MOLE*. ITS DELICATE FLAVOR MAY SURPRISE THOSE PEOPLE WHO ASSUME ALL MEXICAN FOOD IS SPICY. TRY POACHING SHRIMP IN THIS SAUCE.

basics

2 cloves garlic, pan-roasted until browned and soft, then peeled

1 slice (³⁄₄ inch thick) white onion, pan-roasted until browned and soft

¹⁄₄ cup minced fresh cilantro

3 fresh epazote leaves, minced (optional)

¹⁄₄ teaspoon cumin seeds, toasted and freshly ground

¹⁄₂ cup hulled green pumpkin seeds, toasted and freshly ground

2 jalapeño chiles, pan-roasted until blistered and deeply browned, then seeded and deveined

1 ripe tomato, pan-roasted until blistered, deeply browned, and soft

¹⁄₄ teaspoon salt

2 cups chicken broth, or as needed

Place the garlic, onion, cilantro, epazote, cumin, pumpkin seeds, jalapeños, tomato, and salt in a food processor and purée until smooth. In a saucepan, bring the 2 cups broth to a boil, whisk in the purée, and simmer until thickened, about 20 minutes, adding more broth as needed to make a thick sauce. The salsa is best the day it's made, but it can be refrigerated overnight and used the next day.

Makes about 3 cups.

Roasted Corn Salsa

THIS MODERN SOUTHWESTERN SALSA IS THE FIRST RECIPE I EVER PUBLISHED. I STILL LIKE IT, ESPECIALLY WITH WILD MUSHROOM QUESADILLAS (PAGE 66).

3 ears of corn, in their husks

1 tablespoon olive oil

$\frac{1}{2}$ cup roasted, peeled, and diced red bell pepper

1 poblano chile, roasted, peeled, seeded, and diced

3 sun-dried tomatoes, chopped

1 clove garlic, pan-roasted until browned and soft, then peeled and chopped

1 tablespoon minced fresh cilantro

$\frac{1}{4}$ cup chopped sautéed fresh wild mushrooms

1 teaspoon minced *chipotle chile en adobo*

salt

basics

Preheat an oven to 500°F. Place the unhusked ears of corn directly on the oven rack and roast for 5 minutes. Remove from the oven and let cool.

Preheat a broiler or light a grill. Shuck the corn, rub off the silk with your hands or a towel, and brush the ears with the olive oil. Grill or broil the corn, turning as necessary, until it is caramel brown all over, about 5 minutes. Remove from the broiler or grill and let cool until it can be handled. Then, holding each ear upright in a shallow bowl, cut the kernels from the ears. Be careful not to cut into the woody part of the cob.

Add all of the remaining ingredients to the corn, including salt to taste. Mix well and serve immediately.

Makes about 2 cups.

Pico de Gallo

PICO DE GALLO (BEAK OF THE ROOSTER) IS PERHAPS THE MOST COMMON SALSA IN MEXICO, AND ALSO ONE OF THE SIMPLEST TO MAKE. IT IS MADE FROM ONLY FOUR INGREDIENTS, ALL RAW: CHILES, TOMATO, ONION, AND CILANTRO. USE IT BY ITSELF AS A DIP FOR CHIPS OR AS AN ALL-PURPOSE SALSA ON JUST ABOUT ANYTHING.

3 jalapeño chiles, roughly chopped

1 tomato, chopped

1 cup coarsely chopped white onion

¼ cup coarsely chopped fresh cilantro

¼ teaspoon salt

2 tablespoons water

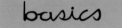

Mix together all the ingredients in a small nonreactive bowl. Let sit for a few minutes to develop the flavors before using. Keep, tightly covered, in the refrigerator for up to 2 days.

Makes about 2 cups.

Pineapple Salsa

HOT, SWEET, AND SASSY. I LOVE THIS SALSA ON ALL
KINDS OF SHELLFISH AND PORK.

$\frac{1}{2}$ **cup finely diced fresh pineapple**

2 tablespoons freshly squeezed lime juice

1 tablespoon freshly squeezed orange juice

1 habanero chile, diced

basics

In a small nonreactive bowl, mix together the pineapple, lime and orange juices, and habanero chile. Cover and let sit in the refrigerator for at least 30 minutes or for up to 2 hours. This salsa is best used the day it's made. **Makes about $\frac{1}{2}$ cup.**

Taqueria Guacamole

THIS SMOOTH, SPICY GUACAMOLE IS MUCH LESS
EXPENSIVE TO MAKE THAN CONVENTIONAL GUA-
CAMOLE. THAT'S WHY IT IS FAVORED BY TAQUERIAS.
IT HAPPENS TO BE MUCH LOWER IN FAT AS WELL.

1 jalapeño chile

3 tablespoons coarsely chopped fresh cilantro

1 avocado, pitted and peeled

¼ teaspoon salt

1 cup water

3 tablespoons diced white onion

Combine all the ingredients except the onion in a food processor and process until very smooth. Pour into a bowl and stir in the onion. Use immediately.

Makes about 2 cups.

Ancho Chile Sauce

This simple, delicious sauce is an easy substitute for the more complex and sophisticated *moles*. Serve this sauce with enchiladas filled with *picadillo* as an entree.

4 tablespoons corn oil

3 ancho chiles

¼ cup boiling water

1 Roma tomato

1 slice (1 inch thick) onion pan-roasted until browned and soft

1 clove garlic, pan-roasted until browned and soft, then peeled

pinch of toasted and freshly ground cumin

¼ teaspoon dried Mexican oregano, toasted

2½ cups chicken broth or water

¼ teaspoon salt

basics

In a skillet over medium heat, warm 2 tablespoons of the oil. When it is hot but not smoking, add the chiles, one or two at a time, and fry until puffed and beginning to brown, 5 to 10 seconds. Shake off the excess oil, transfer the chiles to a bowl, and add the boiling water. Let soak until soft, about 20 minutes.

Meanwhile, place the tomato in a small saucepan and add water to cover. Bring to a boil over high heat, then reduce the heat to low. Simmer, uncovered, until soft, about 10 minutes. Drain and transfer to a blender. Add the chiles and their soaking water, the onion, garlic, cumin, and oregano and purée until smooth.

In a nonstick skillet over medium heat, warm the remaining 2 tablespoons corn oil. Add the purée and fry, stirring occasionally, until bubbly and thickened, about 10 minutes. Transfer to a large, heavy saucepan and add the broth (or water) and salt. Place over medium heat and bring to a simmer, stirring occasionally to prevent sticking. Reduce the heat to low and simmer for 10 minutes. Taste for seasoning. Use at once, or let cool, cover, and refrigerate for up to 5 days.

Makes about 3 cups.

Chipotle Rub

This easy-to-make *recado* adds a smoky complexity to a wide range of foods from corn to pork to seafood and almost anything else.

1 tablespoon corn oil

3 chipotle chiles, seeded and deveined

2 tablespoons kosher salt

1 tablespoon dried Mexican oregano, toasted
   and freshly ground

5 cloves garlic

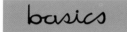 *basics* ·

Place the oil in a sauté pan over medium-high heat. When it is hot but not smoking, add the chiles, one or two at a time, and fry, turning once, until puffed and brown, about 1 minute. Do not let the chiles burn or the chipotle rub will be bitter. Drain the chiles by shaking off the excess oil and set aside until cool and crisp. Discard the oil.

In a spice mill, grind the chiles, in batches, until powdery. Add the chile powder, salt, oregano, and garlic to a food processor and process until you have a shaggy saltlike spice rub. If the mix seems wet, spread it in a thin layer on a dry baking sheet and let it dry out in a cool (150°F) oven for 1 hour or so. Store in a covered container at room temperature indefinitely. Regrind before use, if necessary.

Makes about ½ cup.

Mole Rojo

This slightly sweet *MOLE* surprises many people who expect *MOLE* to be a thick brown "chocolate sauce." I love its rich heat when married to the complex flavor of *PICADILLO*. Customers at Café Marimba also seem to love it; we sell upward of thirty gallons a week. This *MOLE* is also great served over poached chicken as an entrée.

6 ancho chiles

4 guajillo chiles

4 tablespoons corn oil

1 cup boiling water

2 whole cloves

1 teaspoon freshly ground *canela*

½ teaspoon freshly ground black pepper

½ teaspoon dried Mexican oregano, toasted

4 allspice berries

4 cloves garlic, pan-roasted until browned and soft, then peeled

4 Roma tomatoes

1 white onion, thinly sliced

6 cups chicken broth, or as needed

2 ounces Mexican chocolate, broken into pieces

¼ cup sugar

½ teaspoon salt

basics

Seed and devein all the chiles. In a skillet over medium-high heat, warm 2 tablespoons of the oil. When it is hot but not smoking, add the chiles, a few at a time, and cook until puffed and just beginning to brown, 5 to 10 seconds. Shake off the excess oil, transfer the chiles to a bowl, and add the boiling water. Let soak until soft, about 20 minutes. Discard the oil in the skillet.

In a spice mill or mortar, grind together the cloves, *canela*, black pepper, oregano, and allspice. Combine the chiles and their soaking water, the ground spices, and garlic in a blender. Grind until very smooth. You may have to add more water to get the mixture to turn against the blades; continue to add water until the paste turns over smoothly in the blender. You should have a very stiff paste.

Coat a small nonstick pan with 1 tablespoon of the oil and place over medium heat. Add the paste and fry, stirring occasionally, until fragrant, slightly golden on the surface, and very thick (about 20 minutes, or longer if you had to add a lot of water to the blender). You should have a thick, dry, toasty-looking, smooth paste. Transfer to a heavy saucepan and set aside.

Put the tomatoes and onion in a saucepan and add water to cover. Bring to a boil over high heat, then reduce the heat to low. Simmer, uncovered, until the tomatoes and onion are soft, about 10 minutes. Drain, transfer to a blender, and purée until smooth.

Coat the same nonstick pan with the remaining 1 tablespoon oil and place over medium-high heat. Pour the tomato purée into the pan and fry, stirring occasionally, until thick, about 5 minutes. Add to the *mole* paste along with the 6 cups chicken broth. Bring to a simmer over medium heat, whisking occasionally, and simmer, reducing slightly, for 45 minutes.

Whisk in the chocolate, sugar, and salt and simmer for 10 minutes longer; add more chicken broth if the sauce becomes too thick. Check for seasoning, adding more salt or sugar as needed. Use at once, or let cool, cover, and refrigerate for up to 5 days.

Makes about 6 cups.

Mole Amarillo

This pale yellowish red *MOLE* is simple to make and has a compelling, exotic aroma. It is sometimes made with varieties of yellow chiles from Oaxaca such as the *costeño amarillo* or the *chilhuacle amarillo*, but seems to be most often made with the readily obtainable guajillo. This *MOLE* is traditionally simmered together with chicken, green beans, and chayote squash for a delicious stew.

4 tablespoons corn oil

5 guajillo chiles, stemmed and seeded

½ cup boiling water

2 Roma tomatoes

3 tomatillos, husked and rinsed

2 slices (1 inch thick) white onion, pan roasted until browned and soft

4 cloves garlic, pan-roasted until browned and soft, then peeled

4 allspice berries, freshly ground

2 teaspoons toasted and freshly ground cumin

2 whole cloves, freshly ground

1 fresh or 5 dried *hierba santa* leaves

1 teaspoon dried Mexican oregano, toasted

4 ounces fresh corn *masa* for tortillas

6 cups chicken broth

½ teaspoon salt

basics

In a skillet over medium-high heat, warm 2 tablespoons of the oil. When it is hot but not smoking, add the chiles, a couple at a time, and fry until puffed and beginning to brown, 5 to 10 seconds. Shake off the excess oil, transfer the chiles to a bowl, and add the boiling water. Let soak until soft, about 20 minutes. Drain the chiles and set aside.

Meanwhile combine the tomatoes and tomatillos in a small saucepan and add water to cover. Bring to a simmer over high heat, then reduce the heat to low. Simmer, uncovered, until the tomatoes and tomatillos are soft, about 10 minutes. Remove from the heat and drain.

In a blender, combine the chiles, tomatoes, tomatillos, onion, garlic, allspice, cumin, cloves, *hierba santa*, and oregano. Purée until smooth. Heat the remaining 2 tablespoons oil in a large nonstick pan over medium heat. Add the purée and fry until bubbly and thickened, about 10 minutes. Remove from the heat and let cool slightly, then return to the blender. Add the *masa* and a little of the chicken broth and purée until smooth.

Pour the purée and the remaining chicken broth into a large saucepan, add the salt, and place over medium heat. Bring to a simmer, stirring constantly to prevent sticking. Reduce the heat to low and simmer uncovered, stirring occasionally, until the flavors are blended, about 10 minutes. Taste and adjust the seasoning. Use immediately, or let cool, cover, and refrigerate for up to 3 days.

Makes about 7 cups.

Picadillo

This spicy, sweet dish, with its olives, capers, cinnamon, and raisins, seems almost out of place in Mexico. *Picadillo* is originally from Spain. You can see the Moorish influence in the use of sugar. In any event, when you get ground beef in your next Mexican-restaurant enchiladas, this recipe is what they should be making. Versatile *picadillo* can be used as filling for tacos, *chiles rellenos*, *empanaditas*, or anything else your imagination desires.

8 ounces boneless beef chuck

8 ounces boneless pork butt

$\frac{1}{2}$ small white onion, sliced

$\frac{1}{2}$ medium-sized white onion, thickly sliced ($\frac{3}{4}$ inch) and pan-roasted until browned and soft

3 cloves garlic, pan-roasted until browned and soft, then peeled

4 tomatoes, pan-roasted until blistered, deeply browned, and soft

$\frac{1}{2}$ tablespoon freshly ground *canela*

$\frac{1}{4}$ teaspoon dried Mexican oregano, toasted and freshly ground

2 cloves, freshly ground

$\frac{1}{2}$ teaspoon freshly ground black pepper

2 tablespoons olive oil

2 tablespoons drained capers

2 tablespoons coarsely chopped Spanish olives

$\frac{1}{4}$ cup unblanched whole almonds, chopped

2 tablespoons dried currants

$\frac{1}{3}$ teaspoon salt

2 tablespoons sugar

1 tablespoon chopped fresh parsley

basics

Put the beef, pork, and small sliced onion in a large saucepan. Add water to cover the meat and place over medium heat. Bring to a simmer and cook until the meat is falling apart, about 2 hours. Remove from the heat and let cool. Using your fingers, shred the meat, discarding any fat or connective tissue. Reserve the broth.

Place the roasted onion, garlic, tomatoes, *canela*, oregano, cloves, and pepper in a food processor and process to form a coarse purée. In a large nonstick sauté pan over medium heat, warm the olive oil. Add the purée and fry until it thickens slightly, 6 to 8 minutes. Add half of the reserved broth with its fat, the capers, olives, almonds, currants, salt, and sugar. Simmer, uncovered, over medium heat, stirring occasionally, until the mixture begins to thicken, about 20 minutes. Add the rest of the broth and the parsley and cook until the mixture is thick, about 20 minutes more. Taste and adjust the seasonings with salt and sugar.

Use immediately, or let cool, cover, and refrigerate for up to 5 days.

Makes about 4 cups.

Oaxacan Black Beans

These are the best black beans there are. The fragrance of the avocado leaves is exotic, transporting you to a pre-Hispanic Mexico. Once the beans are cooked and puréed, they should be very loose, soft, and perfectly smooth. If you add a little more water and some fried and crumbled pasilla chiles, the beans make a perfect soup. These beans can also be baked in a 300°F oven for about 2 hours.

4 avocado leaves

2 cups dried black beans, picked over

1½ quarts water

1 small white onion, thickly sliced (¾ inch), pan-roasted until browned and soft

4 cloves garlic, pan-roasted until browned and soft, then peeled

¾ teaspoon salt

 ·· *basics*

Put the avocado leaves in a dry skillet over medium heat and toast until browned and fragrant, about 10 seconds. Transfer the leaves to a large pot and add the beans, water, onion, and garlic. Bring to a boil over high heat, lower the heat to a simmer, cover, and cook until very soft, about 1½ hours, adding more water as needed if beans begin to dry.

Drain the cooked beans, reserving the cooking liquid. Working in batches, purée the beans in a blender until smooth, adding just enough of the cooking liquid to allow them to blend. Return to a saucepan and stir in the salt. The mixture should be thick yet pourable. Reheat gently and serve immediately, or let cool, cover, and refrigerate for up to 2 days.

Makes about 4 cups.

Yucatán Variation: Substitute 10 fresh epazote leaves for the avocado leaves and reduce the water to 5 cups. If you can't find epazote, you can substitute 1 teaspoon dried Mexican oregano, although the flavor will not be as distinguished.

Masa for Sopes

THE TRICK TO *SOPES* IS MAKING A DOUGH THAT
REMAINS MOIST AND NEVER GETS TOUGH. SOME OLD
RECIPES USE BEEF MARROW TO SOFTEN THE MASA.
POTATO IS EASIER TO DEAL WITH AND GIVES A GREAT
FLAVOR. THIS SAME DOUGH IS USED FOR MAKING
CHALUPAS.

1 small baking potato
14 ounces fresh corn *masa* for tortillas
$\frac{1}{2}$ teaspoon salt
$\frac{1}{4}$ cup vegetable shortening or lard

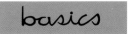 

Preheat an oven to 400°F. Place the potato directly on the oven rack. Bake until soft throughout, about 45 minutes. Remove from the oven, prick, and let cool slightly, then cut in half and scoop out the flesh. Pass the flesh through a potato ricer or sieve into a bowl and let cool completely.

Add the *masa*, salt, and shortening (or lard) to the cooled potato and knead in the bowl until smooth. Use immediately or refrigerate overnight.

Makes about 1 pound.

Sweet Potato Tortillas

These unusual tortillas are certainly not traditional, but they are fun to make and taste great. Try serving them with game or *mole* sauces.

1 medium-sized sweet potato
2 cups all-purpose flour
2 tablespoons unsalted butter
½ teaspoon salt

basics

Preheat an oven to 400°F. Place the sweet potato directly on the oven rack. Bake until soft throughout, about 45 minutes. Remove from the oven, prick, and let cool slightly. Cut in half lengthwise and scoop out the orange flesh into a food processor. Let cool completely. Add the flour, butter, and salt to the processor and process until smooth.

Transfer the dough to a lightly floured work surface and knead briefly; it should be soft and pliable. If the dough seems too sticky, add a little more flour. Using a rolling pin or a pasta machine, roll out the dough in 1 or 2 long strips; it should be as thin as possible. Using a 5-inch plate as a template, cut out rounds; you should have 8 in all.

Preheat a dry *comal* or griddle over medium-high heat until a drop of water sizzles on the surface. Cook the tortillas on the first side until the edges lighten and begin to curl slightly, about 3 minutes. Using a spatula, turn and cook on the second side until they color and puff slightly. Continue to cook, turning as needed, until both sides are covered with brownish black dots and the tortillas are cooked through, about 3 minutes longer. Transfer the cooked tortillas to a clean kitchen towel and wrap them to keep them warm. To keep them longer than 20 minutes, wrap the towel in aluminum foil and keep warm in a 150°F oven. To keep them longer than 1 hour, let them cool and reheat over an open flame or on a hot *comal*, turning from side to side until hot and blistered.

Makes 8 tortillas.

Tlayudas with Cheese

Corn Tortillas Using Fresh Masa

WORKING WITH FRESH CORN *MASA* IS UNEXPECTEDLY EASY FOR THOSE PEOPLE ACCUSTOMED TO WORKING WITH WHEAT-FLOUR DOUGHS. CORN *MASA* HAS NO GLUTEN, SO THE DOUGH DOES NOT STRETCH OR RESIST WHEN YOU FORM IT. I THINK OF FORMING IT AS SORT OF LIKE WORKING WITH MODELING CLAY. IT WILL READILY TAKE ANY SHAPE YOU WISH. TO MAKE TORTILLAS, ALL YOU DO IS PRESS OUT THE DOUGH AND COOK IT. IT'S THAT EASY.

1 pound fresh corn *masa*

basics

Knead the *masa* briefly. It should be smooth and soft to the touch. If it seems dry, add a bit of water. Taste the *masa*: if it seems sour, discard it. Divide the *masa* into 6 equal-sized balls. Place each ball in the center of a 7-inch square of waxed paper. Flatten the ball slightly with the palm of your hand. Put a second sheet of waxed paper of the same size on top. Place in the press or between 2 books and press down hard, using your body weight to flatten the *masa*. Open the press, or remove the top book, and remove the tortilla, keeping it between the sheets of paper.

To cook the tortillas, preheat a dry *comal* or griddle over medium-high heat until a drop of water sizzles on the surface. Take 1 tortilla and remove the top sheet of waxed paper. Lay the tortilla on the griddle waxed paper side up and press down lightly on the edges. Peel off the paper, pulling to the side rather than straight up. Let the tortilla cook on the first side until the edges lighten and begin to curl slightly, about 3 minutes. Using a spatula, turn the tortilla and cook on the second side until it begins to color. Continue to cook, turning as needed, until both sides are covered with brownish black dots and the tortilla is cooked through, about 3 minutes longer.

As the tortillas are cooked, wrap them in a clean kitchen towel. If you wish to keep the tortillas warm for more than 20 minutes, wrap the towel in aluminum foil and put it in a 150°F oven. Tortillas are best when they are first made. Holding them warm for too long will cause them to toughen. If you want to keep them longer than 1 hour, let them cool and reheat over an open flame or on a hot *comal*, turning from side to side until hot and blistered.

Makes 6 tortillas.

Mail-order Sources

The ingredients commonly used for making Mexican food are available in supermarkets across the country. Many of them are found in the ethnic-foods section, which often contains a large number of Latin American products. The produce section carries fresh and dried chiles, fresh cilantro, and tomatillos in season.

Still, some ingredients, such as certain dried chiles and epazote, can be harder to find, although most are no farther away than your local Mexican or Latin American grocery. Farmers' markets are another excellent resource, especially for fresh and dried chiles. If you still have trouble locating certain items, this is a list of companies, including my own (Marimba Products at my restaurant, Café Marimba), that will mail order ingredients.

MARIMBA PRODUCTS
2317 CHESTNUT STREET
SAN FRANCISCO, CA 94123
TELEPHONE: 415-347-0111
FAX: 415-347-3823
CATALOG AVAILABLE

A FULL LINE OF DRIED CHILES AND HERBS AND SPICES, INCLUDING EPAZOTE, *HIERBA SANTA*, AND AVOCADO LEAF, AND A WIDE RANGE OF PREPARED SALSAS, *RECADOS*, AND MOLES.

IT'S ABOUT THYME
P. O. BOX 878
MANCHACA, TX 78652
TELEPHONE: 512-280-1192
CATALOG AVAILABLE

AN AMAZING ARRAY OF HERB PLANTS THAT ARE SHIPPED TO CUSTOMERS BY UPS. BUY *HIERBA SANTA* AND EPAZOTE, BOTH OF WHICH GROW WELL IN MILD CLIMATES.

LOS CHILEROS DE NUEVO MEXICO
P. O. BOX 6215
SANTA FE, NM 87502
TELEPHONE: 505-471-6967
CATALOG AVAILABLE

SPECIALIZES IN NEW MEXICO FOOD PRODUCTS AND CARRIES ALL TYPES OF DRIED CHILES.

LA PALMA
2884 24TH STREET
SAN FRANCISCO, CA 94110
TELEPHONE: 415-647-1500
NO CATALOG

A TERRIFIC SHOP IN THE TRADITION OF *BARRIO* MARKETS ACROSS THE UNITED STATES. IT IS BEST TO GO IN PERSON AND DEFINITELY WORTH THE VISIT. THEY WILL SHIP, BUT ARE A BIT RELUCTANT TO DO SO.

TIERRA VEGETABLES
13684 CHALK HILL ROAD
HEALDSBURG, CA 95448
TELEPHONE: 707-433-5666
PRICE LIST AVAILABLE

THIS SMALL FARMER GROWS MANY CHILE VARIETIES WITHOUT THE USE OF PESTICIDES, HERBICIDES, OR FUMIGATES.

GLEN BURNS FARMS
16158 HILLSIDE CIRCLE
MONTVERDE, FL 34756
TELEPHONE: 407-469-4490

CALL THIS FARM IF YOU AREN'T HAVING ANY LUCK FINDING HUITLACOCHE. THIS IS WHERE CAFÉ MARIMBA BUYS IT.

Equivalents

The exact equivalents in the following tables have been rounded for convenience.

Oven Temperatures

F	Celsius	Gas	F	Celsius	Gas	F	Celsius	Gas
250	120	½	350	180	4	450	230	8
275	140	1	375	190	5	475	240	9
300	150	2	400	200	6			
325	160	3	425	220	7			

Liquids

US		Metric	UK	US		Metric	UK
2	tbl	30 ml	1 fl oz	¾	cup	180 ml	6 fl oz
¼	cup	60 ml	2 fl oz	1	cup	250 ml	8 fl oz
⅓	cup	80 ml	3 fl oz	1½	cups	375 ml	12 fl oz
½	cup	125 ml	4 fl oz	2	cups	500 ml	16 fl oz
⅔	cup	160 ml	5 fl oz	4	cups/1 qt	1 l	32 fl oz

Length Measures

US/UK	Metric	US/UK	Metric	US/UK	Metric
⅛ in	3 mm	3 in	7.5 cm	8 in	20 cm
¼ in	6 mm	4 in	10 cm	9 in	23 cm
½ in	12 mm	5 in	13 cm	10 in	25 cm
1 in	2.5 cm	6 in	15 cm	11 in	28 cm
2 in	5 cm	7 in	18 cm	12 in/1 ft	30 cm

Weights

US/UK	Metric	US/UK	Metric
1 oz	30 g	10 oz	315 g
2 oz	60 g	12 oz (¼ lb)	375 g
3 oz	90 g	14 oz	440 g
4 oz (¼ lb)	125 g	16 oz (1 lb)	500 g
5 oz (⅓ lb)	155 g	1½ lb	750 g
6 oz	185 g	2 lb	1 kg
7 oz	220 g	3 lb	1.5 kg
8 oz (½ lb)	250 g		

Units

US/UK	Metric
oz = ounce	g = gram
lb = pound	kg = kilogram
in = inch	mm = millimeter
ft = foot	cm = centimeter
tbl = tablespoon	ml = milliliter
fl oz = fluid ounce	l = liter

index

Wild Mushrooms in Salsa Verde